EVITA

SAINT
OR SINNER?

EVITA

SAINT
OR SINNER?

W. A. Harbinson

BⓍXTREE

First published in Britain in this format 1996 by
Boxtree Limited,
Broadwall House, 21 Broadwall, London SE1 9PL

10 9 8 7 6 5 4 3 2

A CIP catalogue record for this book is available from
the British Library

ISBN: 0 7522 0200 6

Cover design by Shoot That Tiger!
Front cover photograph: Associated Press

Typeset in Sabon by SX Composing DTP, Rayleigh, Essex
Printed and bound in Great Britain by
Cox & Wyman Ltd, Reading, Berkshire

Contents

Acknowledgements

Personal thanks to: Rexton S. Bunnett and John Basham for theatre research; Tanya Harbinson for film research; Ken Welsh and Mark Little of *Lookout* magazine for information regarding Juan Perón in Spain and the career of Antonio Banderas; Adam Webb of World Wide Web (B) for culling the Internet; the Hans Tasiemka Agency for press cuttings; Martin Atcherley and the staff of the library at Canning House for research regarding Argentina.

I am indebted to the following books: *The Woman With A Whip* (Garden City, New York, 1952) by Mary Main; *Bloody Precedent* (Random House, New York, 1952) by Fleur Cowles; *Perón: His Rise and Fall* (Cresset Press, London, 1957) by Owen Frank; *Eva Perón* (W.H. Allen & Co, London, 1978) by John Barnes; *Eva Perón* (André Deutsch, London, 1980) by Nicholas Fraser and Navarro Marysa; *Evita – The Legend of Eva Perón 1919–1952* (Elm Tree Books/Hamish Hamilton, London, 1978) by Andrew Lloyd Webber and Tim Rice (main text by the latter); *The Musicals of Andrew Lloyd Webber* (Virgin, London, 1995) by Keith Richmond; *Madonna: Lucky Star* (Columbus Books, London, 1985) by Michael McKenzie; *Madonna: The Biography* (Sidgwick & Jackson, London, 1989) by Robert Matthew-Walker; *Madonna Revealed* (Smyth Gryphon Ltd, London, 1991) by Douglas Thompson.

Part One

DEATH AND DEIFICATION

Without fanaticism one cannot accomplish anything.
                                    – Evita Perón

Chapter One

When one of the world's great lovers, Rudolph Valentino, died in the summer of 1926, the then-unheard-of sum of 50,000 mourners turned out in Manhattan to pay their final respects.

When another of the world's great lovers, Dona Maria Eva Duarte de Perón – better known to the people of Argentina as Evita, the Lady of Hope, the Lady of Compassion, and officially named Spiritual Chief of the Nation – died in the summer of 1952, some 700,000 Argentinians turned out in Buenos Aires, demonstrated passionately in the streets, and lost themselves so completely in their grief that sixteen of them were killed, 3,900 ended up in various hospitals, and thousands more had to receive first aid.

To feed these multitudes, the army had to set up twenty-four field kitchens, giving away sandwiches, oranges and coffee. In an attempt to quell the mobs that howled and crushed one another in the Avenida de Mayo, other soldiers were forced to offer batons instead of nourishment. In the Avenida de Mayo itself, placed there at an estimated cost of $2 million, approximately 8,300 wreaths had been laid, some of them piled thirty feet high.

Argentine newspapers, normally limited to six or eight pages daily by newsprint shortages, were told by the government that they could now use all the paper they wanted in reporting the career and death of the beloved Evita. Radio stations cut their scheduled pro-

3

grammes and played solemn music instead. The Argentine Press Office rebroadcast the announcement of Evita's death at fifteen-minute intervals. More first-aid stations sprang up in the streets for the many jostling, weeping multitudes.

The following day, Evita was exposed to her people. In a flowing white tunic, her blonde hair (dyed) splayed over a white pillow, she lay in state in a silver-trimmed cedar coffin with a full-length glass top, in the National Congress Hall. Day and night, often in torrential rain, miles-long queues waited in the black-shrouded streets to see her.

Two million filed past Evita's bier in the first few days. They filed slowly past the beautiful blonde hair, past the once delectable body now shrunken in death, past those brightly painted lips that on posters and hoardings had suggested fellatio to the fevered imaginations of her most macho subjects. These macho subjects now shuffled past, holding their caps in their rough workers' hands. They gazed down at the 'little whore', the glamorous actress, their benefactress; at the poor girl who had come from the pampas to enrich their poor lives. And, shuffling past her, they also shuffled past Juan Domingo Perón, the President himself, now the bereaved husband, big and bulky, wearing a black tie and armband, his dark, overfed, latent schoolboy's face gazing down on his deceased other half.

The *descamisados*, Evita's poor 'shirtless ones', shuffled past with their heavy wives trembling by their sides. Dressed all in black, these women were wringing their hands and sobbing and holding on to each other. They glanced with awe at the President and saw the tears on his cheeks. They saw the people all around him, but these people were not so familiar. Amongst them were Evita's mother, her three sisters, the Governor of Baires, the Minister of Communications, the Minister of Technical Affairs, the Minister of Political Affairs and Raul Apold, Under-Secretary of Press, and Atilio Renzi, Evita's personal secretary. The *descamisados* possibly also saw Jose Espejo, the boss of Evita's unions, who would soon be arrested by Perón and never be seen again; and Evita's dissolute brother, Juan Ramon Duarte, who had been her personal aide and who would soon resign suddenly and 'commit suicide' in a manner not easily explained. No matter: the *descamisados* shuffled past. They saw their 'madonna' in the coffin, the public grief of the President, and then they moved back out into the streets, to rejoin the other massed thousands.

Two million grew to three million. The queues seemed never to end. In the chaotic streets some were actually crushed to death and many more were injured. In the open-air clinics people lay on camp beds, pale and bewildered, many covered in blood, succumbing to exhaustion or starvation after days in the open. And at night, beneath the huge, black-draped portrait of Evita that dominated the Avenida de Mayo, the blaze of countless torches held aloft by those mourning illuminated the stacked, garish flowers.

The mourning continued. The country came to a virtual standstill. Factories, slaughteryards, offices and schools stood silent and empty. Across the nation they were renaming streets, institutions, an entire county and the city of La Plata in Evita's memory. Buildings and lampposts were draped in black and Masses were celebrated, until, after two hysterical weeks, Evita's body was transferred via a gun carriage

5

towed by fifty men and women in a pageant reminiscent of Cecil B. DeMille, along a one-mile funeral route packed with weeping thousands, to the headquarters of the General Confederation of Labour (CGT) where, resting in the glass-topped coffin in an immense horseshoe of white and mauve orchids, Santa (Saint) Evita's body was to remain until a mausoleum, 150 feet taller than the Statue of Liberty, could be built in downtown Buenos Aires.

So great was the grief of Evita's husband, President Juan Domingo Perón, that on 17 October, the anniversary of the Perónist revolution, he dedicated the day to Evita. Argentina subsequently exploded with an avalanche of commemorative busts, medals, pictures, records, pennants, keyrings and postage stamps. Thousands of copies of Evita's book, *La Razon di mi Vida* (*The Reason for My Life*) were distributed. More streets, schools, squares, even rivers and mountains, were named after her. And every night, on the radio, the main news bulletin was preceded by the words: 'It is now 20.25, the hour when Eva Perón entered immortality.'

Plans were drawn up for her tomb. The exterior was to be adorned with sixteen statues of the 'deity' reposing in the silver sarcophagus inside. A 140-foot-tall statue of a *descamisado* (its construction to be financed by the extraction of one day's earnings from every lowly paid 'shirtless one' in employment) would tower on the roof.

Plans were made to have the body embalmed.

The religious fervour of the mourning continued. While the people still wept in the streets, the Minister of Public Health, Ramon Carillo, ordered a 220lb candle, the same height as Evita (5ft 2in), to be

6

installed in the Ministry and lit for an hour on the 26th day of every month, thus ensuring that this symbol of Evita's death would remain for posterity. Not to be outdone, the Union of Workers and Employees of the Food Industry cabled a request to Pope Pius XII to canonise Evita. The request was denied.

While schoolchildren were receiving prizes for poems and essays praising the deceased and being told that Evita, like Christ, had died because she had 'kissed the ill, the lepers, the consumptives', the newly formed Association of Friends of Evita was basing its organisation's principles on the simple credo: 'What would Christ have done without His disciples?'

Not content with this, various senators in the Congress were waxing eloquent as to how the First Lady of Argentina had combined the best virtues of Catherine the Great of Russia, Queen Elizabeth I of England and Isabella of Spain. Having thus aligned Evita with both Christ and the greatest ladies in history, the government then announced that 26 July, the day of her death, would be observed for 'the rest of history' as a day of national mourning. And good *Perónistas*, the party ruled, would wear black ties at future party meetings . . . *forever*.

It did not pass unnoticed that both Evita and Christ had died at thirty-three years of age.

Nor that Evita, like Christ, had achieved sainthood.

Chapter Two

Three years later, President Juan Domingo Perón, still wearing black in mourning for his deceased wife, was banning photographs of himself and a group of high-school girls of the Union de Estudiantes Secundarios, the 124-acre presidential estate he had turned over to them for their games. The reason for the banning was that one of the girls, then only sixteen years old, was rumoured to have become his mistress two or three years earlier – a story that the 'shirtless ones' were all too willing to believe, given their fondness for the memory of Evita, their conviction about Juan Perón's singular sexual proclivities, and the rumour that Perón had, earlier that year, secretly married the nineteen-year-old Laura del Solar.

At roughly the same time, the esteemed but, in this instance, certainly naïve Herbert L. Matthews of the *New York Times* was assuring his readers that the Argentine President's fondness for playing games with adolescent girls was nothing other than a 'normally innocent and politically astute policy to gain more popularity' and that, since the death of his beloved Evita, 'there have been no other women and there surely will be none.' Matthews went on to assure his readers that Perón's popularity was undiminished by Evita's death, that his power was 'supreme' and that his position as President of Argentina was 'unchallengeable' – an unfortunate claim.

For some time Perón had been quarrelling with the church, the military clique and the wealthy. His argument with the church soon made him the first, and so far only, twentieth-century head of state to be excommunicated by the Vatican. Worse was to come, however. On 16 July 1955, three years after Evita's death, elements of the navy bombed May Square and the presidential mansion (the Casa Rosada). Perón's supporters started burning churches in retaliation. By September the military were in power again and Perón, hiding on a Paraguayan gunboat on the Plata River, was scribbling to his sixteen-year-old sweetheart: 'You are all I have left now the workers have deserted me . . . I miss you every day . . . Many kisses and many desires . . .' and signing the note, 'Papi', Argentine for 'Daddykins'.

While Perón, still hiding on the gunboat, was scribbling this adolescent nonsense to his adolescent mistress, the more divisive passions within the country had reached the state where everything that bore the name 'Perón' or 'Evita' was being destroyed, including posters, statues and Evita's beloved Children's Palace. Meanwhile, investigators working for the new regime were exposing Perón as a sixty-year-old libertine who, in the acidulous words of *Time*, 'liked his girls young, his gadgets golden and his plunder plentiful'. Included in the rather sordid revelations about the 'people's' President was the fact that Perón had stashed away enormous wealth in various overseas banks and had led a private life of extraordinary luxury.

Evidence of the lifestyle of the protector of the *descamisados* came in the shape of at least five dwellings, including the presidential estate at Olivos, an exclusive Buenos Aires suburb where Perón ('Just call me Pocho!') often went to join his adolescent girls in basketball, sailboat racing and skating; or to award wallets containing 500-peso notes to graduates (all female, all adolescent) of the classes in dancing, gymnastics and drama.

Among those pupils was Nelida Rivas, the fourteen-year-old, green-eyed janitor's daughter whom Perón made his mistress and to whom he gave jewels from his late wife's collection, as well as 'poodles, perfume, and a nice little concrete house in the suburbs with her folks'.

Also found by the investigators was a third holiday residence in the pampas south of Buenos Aires, fitted out with bearskin rugs and a fencing court. A fourth residence was an apartment atop an eight-storey building where, in 'boudoirs lined with mirrors', the President enjoyed himself with the now seventeen-year-old Nelida. Closets were crammed with suits, uniforms, jackets and riding boots.

The fifth house, a two-storey Buenos Aires bungalow at 2102 Teodoro Garcia Street in the fashionable suburb of Belgrano, turned out to be a veritable goldmine. Included in the incredible collection were cigarette, jewellery and bon-bon boxes, clocks and watches, coins of various countries, spoons and bowls, toilet sets, ashtrays, and a gold-plated telephone with ivory ear- and mouthpieces. The house had at least ten television sets. Dozens of mink, sable and other luxurious fur coats were found in a deep freeze. There were two hundred suits and eighty-three pairs of shoes. Downstairs was a well-stocked bar under the lewd motto: 'Someone always gets assaulted when a poor man has some fun.' Also downstairs was a huge gold elephant with an enormous emerald – said to be the second largest in the world – embedded in its forehead. Other treasures included precious rugs, tapestries and pictures, as well as an extraordinary collection of paintings, including works by Rembrandt and Velázquez. The basement garage held two of Perón's sixteen cars of every high-priced foreign make. In various safes, vaults and drawers the investigators found close to $20 million in cash.

Obviously conscious of the politics of Argentina and of his own, always precarious, part in them, Perón also had a bomb shelter, which was joined by a secret panel to the ground-floor press room of his own downtown publishing house. An underground vault lined with rosewood, the bomb shelter contained a bedroom, numerous pairs of silk pyjamas, an emergency supply of oxygen, and a 'wall safe big enough to walk into'. Behind one of the walls was another long underground escape tunnel, which led to the office building next door.

While all of this was being uncovered, and while revolution still raged in the streets of Buenos Aires, Juan Domingo Perón, the recent President of Argentina, lover and husband to the revered Evita, was allowed to leave the gunboat on the Plata River and fly off to political exile in Paraguay.

Chapter Three

In 1956, when the new Argentine regime's National Investigating Committee had submitted their report on corruption during the Perón era, they revealed, amongst other items withheld for possible future court proceedings, that Perón had cheated his mother-in-law out of half of her bequest from the late Evita Perón; that he had probably arranged the assassination of Evita's brother, Juan Duarte; that he had arranged the arrest and subsequent disappearance of Jose Espejo, the boss of Evita's beloved unions; that he had lavished millions on the clubs of his Union of High School Students, favouring teenage girls in all such cases; that he had given car import licences worth thousands of dollars to various of his friends; and that both he and his revered wife Evita, Spiritual Chief to the Nation, had stashed away a mass of pilfered wealth in unnamed Swiss banks.

By 1962, ten years after the death of Evita Perón, the keys to a Swiss bank vault in which Evita had deposited cash and jewels worth $25 million had been hunted on and off by both the investigators of the new regime in Argentina and the indefatigable Juan Perón himself.

The assassination of Evita's brother, Juan Duarte, was directly related to this chase.

Shortly after Evita's death, Juan Perón had learned that his wife had for three years been systematically dispatching suitcases full of jewellery, cash and art objects to Switzerland, using for this purpose two women, the first an unknown secretary, the second

Delia Parodi, a Congresswoman. Evita's dissolute brother, Juan Duarte, at this time still trusted by Perón, was sent in company with Hector Campora, a Perón Congressman, to Geneva, to find out exactly how much Evita had hidden in the bank vaults and what had happened to the actual keys. Reportedly they both returned without success.

In April 1953, Juan Duarte was betrayed by Maliza Zini, one of many actresses whose company he had kept in Buenos Aires. It was never known what she had said, but some days later Duarte was found with a bullet in his brain. Although the death was treated officially as suicide, a police surgeon later let it be known that the bullet had been fired from such a distance as to rule this out. Also, some of Perón's agents had ransacked Duarte's apartment and it was common knowledge that the object of the search was the keys to Evita Perón's safety vault.

Those keys were never located.

In exile, Perón did not starve. When the Revolution came and forced him out of Argentina, Perón possessed £430,000 belonging to the Eva Perón Foundation; a ranch worth £261,000; two apartment buildings in Buenos Aires; a £38,000 house; a smaller country estate in Cordoba; shares worth £230,000 in a ranch near Buenos Aires; and £19,000 in shares in Uruguay.

All of this came from the *descamisados*, who had revered Juan Perón and, even more so, the saintly Evita.

During the eighteen years following the death of Evita, the deposed Juan Perón wandered restlessly across Paraguay, Nicaragua, Venezuela, the Dominican Republic and Portugal, eventually settling in Madrid with another woman much younger than himself, the flamenco dancer Isabel Martinez. With her he dreamed and schemed of a return to glory.

While Perón was thus engaged, his dead wife, Evita, was being resurrected and again deified in the hearts and minds of the people of Argentina.

A bizarre fate had overtaken the corpse of Evita. Embalmed at a cost of $100,000, her body, in its silk-lined coffin, was stolen from its temporary resting place in Labour Confederation headquarters in 1955 by agents of the new Argentine president, General Pedro Aramburu, placed in a coffin, dumped in the back of an army lorry, and driven off into the night.

From that moment on the whereabouts of Eva Perón, now Saint Evita – whose remains could be used as a powerful symbol for or against any existing government – became a matter of almost feverish concern and conjecture throughout the Argentine and the whole of Latin America. There were rumours that she had been incinerated and that her ashes had been strewn over the Plata River; that the body was in Chile with Evita's widowed mother and two sisters; that Evita was not in fact dead, but had been kidnapped by Perón and now lived with him in exile in Paraguay. For eighteen long years such rumours proliferated until eventually Evita, once a poor girl and 'little whore', became a legend and a memory of hope to the suppressed of the Argentine.

In April 1971, when the body of Evita Perón reappeared and was delivered with great ceremony to the then 74-year-old but still ambitious Juan Perón, there was only one mystery left unresolved.

What made Evita, the cause of so much corruption, intrigue and violence, a legend of such saintly proportions?

Part Two

THE RISE AND FALL OF EVITA PERÓN

*For many years I have had a limitless quantity of
illusions and dreams. I felt most deeply that the
anguish, the grief and the sadness of our people
could not be eternal.*

– Evita

Chapter Four

To be a saint one must first be a human being. The one-room brick house in Los Toldos is now a wreck being used as a store room. The corrugated iron walls are gradually collapsing over the patio at the back and grass sprouts wildly from the flat roof. Back in 1919 it was habitable but hardly much better. The most desolate of pampas small towns, Los Toldos was built on the site of an Indian camp, 150 miles west of Buenos Aires, the low, flat-fronted, dusty houses symmetrical with the flat monotony of the prairies and surrounded by dirt streets and whitewashed *paraiso* trees.

Into this vast silence, in the early morning of 7 May 1919, was born the child Maria Eva Duarte, the fifth of the five illegitimate children of Juan Duarte and Juana Ibarguren, who lived in the *estancia* La Union. Since this was Tragic Week, when striking workers were massacred by the army, there was perhaps a certain aptness to the birth.

Eva's father, Juan Duarte, rented the ranch at La Union, close to Los Toldos, and lived there with Juana, a local peasant girl. Shortly after Eva's birth, her mother took the family to live in Los Toldos and it was there, in an adobe farmhouse, with chickens and goats and earthen floors, that Eva was to spend her growing years.

Stretching 600 miles from the city of Buenos Aires, the pampas is an area of sandy hills, fertile prairies and marshy lowlands criss-crossed by rambling rivers. Though its wide variety of climates and soils enables it to produce an abundance of wheat and corn (maize), sugar cane, olives, tobacco, tea and cotton, it was, until the middle of the 19th century, a poor region, given over to cattle breeding and mule breeding. However, with the coming of the railway, progress in ocean transport, and the introduction of British beef cattle – Aberdeen Angus, Hereford and Shorthorn, as well as French Charolais – the raising of livestock became the main source of the country's wealth and the farmers of the region did not suffer. Though the labour these men performed was hard and isolating, with little to distract them during the long, lonely days when they rode with the herds or worked the land, the money was there for the taking and many of them prospered.

Eva's father, Juan Duarte, was not one of them. Initially, however, he was certainly not poor. Renting the farm at Los Toldos, he had peons – members of the landless agricultural classes – working for him and was proud of the fact that he possessed the most up-to-date, expensive farm machinery. Another sign of his relative prosperity is that, though living on the farm with Juana Ibarguren and her children, including Eva, he had a legal wife, by whom he had other children, living in another farm in the nearby market town of Chivilcoy.

Described as an 'indolent, agreeable, attractive' man, he tended little to the farm, gradually let it deteriorate, and eventually accrued more debts than he could handle. First the peons went, then the machinery, until eventually, sadly, there was nothing. The indolent Juan Duarte now had to search for a poor living in a very bleak landscape.

Thus it was that early in her life, Eva Duarte learnt the nature of humiliating poverty, acute boredom and grinding frustration. The days were long in Los Toldos, the land was flat and empty, and the silence that surrounded the household made it seem like a prison. Few people departed, visitors rarely arrived, and the richness of the pampas was now beyond the reach of the unfortunate Duartes.

Nor were they aided by the rigid Argentine caste system that divided the wealthy from the poor. Not only were the Duartes poor, they were also bastard children, the fruits of Juan Duarte's unsanctified liaison with the peasant girl, Juana. In the eyes of the other villagers, Juana was a *casa chica* (the 'other wife') and someone to be pointedly avoided. For this reason, Eva and her four sisters were looked upon as 'brats' and often prevented from associating with the other children of the village.

The sense of rejection that was instilled in young Eva by this was something she would never forget and certainly never forgive. Indeed, she would always nurture a secret resentment and the need for revenge, as eventually the Oligarchy, the ruling classes of Buenos Aires, would find out to their cost.

Young Eva's awareness of the privileges of the rich could only have been heightened by the sight of the *estancia*, the village squire's home, with its 'cool courtyard and magnificent rooms' filled with music and laughter. The owner of the hacienda, who also possessed great herds of cattle, hired and fired the gauchos, or cowboys, and had total power over the village, must have seemed almost godlike to the small girl. Given that this god appeared not to recognise Eva's existence, that he and his family could only sneer at the sight of her, it is reasonable to assume that at a very early age her awe would have been mixed with resentment and the need to right the wrongs being done to her. Indeed, she came to hate the rich with a venom that stemmed from the humiliations of her childhood and eventually warped her every emotion.

'I believed that poor people existed as naturally as grass and that the rich were as natural as trees. Then one day a labourer told me that the poor existed because the rich were too rich; and this revelation had a very strong impression on me.'

The other poor were the gauchos, who rode constantly through the village. Wearing nothing but ponchos and motheaten trousers, with jangling spurs strapped to their bare feet, these sunscorched, laconic, tough 'cowboys of the pampas' were the first 'shirtless ones' she ever knew. Locally they were known as 'los paisanos' and they worked from dawn to dusk for practically nothing. Now obsolete and romanticised in Argentinian literature as men of nobility, selflessness and courage, they were, when Eva was a child, widely scorned as drinkers and shiftless vagabonds. Given their tough, chauvinistic nature, that insularity bred from their long, lonely days on the prairies, it is likely that they, too, either ignored or mocked the little bastard, Eva Duarte. Certainly, in later years, when Eva had found fame and fortune, she would not so much feel sympathy for the poor as blinding, abiding hatred for the rich.

'There are rich and there are poor,' she would say, 'and the odd thing is that the existence of the poor pains me less than the knowledge that at the same time others are rich.'

The flame of Eva's rage would be fanned by her mother. While Eva's father was a conservative, accepting the status quo despite his dire circumstances, her mother was instinctively a radical. Independent and strong-minded, she was resentful of her position in this country that treated women as second-class citizens and she therefore instilled in Eva her own drive and self-conviction, a refusal to give in to negative circumstances. It was this influence, combined with the awareness of her illegitimacy and low standing, that turned Eva into a determined, self-serving force.

Another feeling of resentment, this time against men in general, sprang from the fact that her father had a legal wife and children, that they were more respected than the Duartes, and that he was often away from home in Los Toldos, visiting his 'real' family in the town of Chivilcoy. From this, Eva would come to see that the Argentine male was inclined to view women as mere chattels, to be used for physical pleasure and moral support while being denied personal freedom and pride. This, also, was something she would never forget.

Thus, at a very early age, she developed hatred for the rich and contempt for male chauvinism. She also learned early that people could use and could *be* used and decided that she must not be one of the latter. Indeed, though Eva was the youngest of the five sisters, the second youngest girl, Erminda, felt that Eva had always been older than her years and was in many ways the strongest, most mature member of the family.

'She had a much stronger personality,' Erminda says, 'and people thought we were twins, even though

I was two years older than her . . . Her temperament made up for my years . . . She always had this thing: she always gave orders. Everyone was glad to obey her. She knew how to make herself obeyed, either by being nice or by being tough.'

This trait – getting what she wanted by being nice or by being tough – would stand Eva in good stead in the future.

At primary school in Los Toldos, Eva was a relatively bright but unexceptional pupil. Though seemingly bored with her studies, she adored appearing in the school plays and, like most of the other girls, was obsessed with film magazines and the exciting world beyond the pampas – in Buenos Aires and Hollywood. Her desire to become an actress began then and was nurtured by the movie magazines that she begged, borrowed and stole from her friends because her father could not afford to buy them. She spent hours poring over the magazines, mesmerised by the glamorous pictures, and imagining herself living the life of the movie stars. She could do it, she was absolutely convinced, if she could only make her escape from Los Toldos and the vast, desolate pampas. It was a thought to sustain her.

The dream of becoming an actress, preferably a movie star, could only have been heightened by the increasing poverty of her existence (the family resources, not good to begin with, were now dwindling rapidly) and out of the need to escape from the seemingly hopeless future represented by the world's end of Los Toldos. This 'drab island in a rolling ocean of grass' would have encouraged her large brown eyes to search the horizon for escape and adventure.

Rafael Reta, who now lives on a small farm on the

edge of what was once the Duarte ranch, remembers that for some years things had been going well for the Duarte family, but that in the middle twenties, just before Juan Duarte's death, there was a drought which, combined with Duarte's increasing lack of interest in the farm, robbed him of his few remaining pesos. The family's poverty was now absolute, there was no light on the horizon, and each day little Eva must have gazed at the nearby hacienda and burned with her growing resentment of the wealthy.

In the event, a change of scenery came sooner than expected, though in a most brutal, unexpected manner.

In 1926, when Eva was only seven, her father was killed in a car crash. As Duarte had been an 'agreeable, attractive' man, his loss must have been a considerable shock to her. Her pain would not have been eased by the fact that his body was not brought home, but instead delivered for burial to the legal family in Chivilcoy. To make matters worse, when Eva, with her mother, sisters and brothers, attended the funeral, they were greeted as the 'bastard family' of Juan Duarte, herded apart, kept out of the cemetery until the burial was over, then rudely snubbed by the legitimate offspring.

Again, this was something that Eva would neither forget nor forgive – another grudge on her lengthening list of grievances against the contemptible middle classes.

With Juan Duarte's death, life became more difficult for the whole family. Luckily, because Duarte had been a member of the local ruling conservative caste, Señora Duarte received financial aid from the local party. They also found employment for the eldest daughter, Elisa, in the post office in Junin, the nearest town in the province of Buenos Aires.

It was then common in Argentina for single or widowed women to accept the 'protection' of a man of means, becoming his *casa chica* in return for financial security. It was therefore no accident that Señora Duarte was eventually aided by a wealthy 'protector' of the local Radical Party and, with his help, was soon able to open a boarding house in Junin. Determined and capable, she turned the boarding house into a profitable venture and married off two of her daughters: Elisa to Major Alfredo Arrieta, an officer in the Argentine Army; and Blanca (an attractive girl with the blonde hair that dark Eva bitterly envied) to Justo Rodriguez, a promising lawyer. When Erminda, Eva's favourite sister, then married Orlando Bertolini, who operated the lift in the Town Hall of Vincente Lopez, Eva's future must have seemed even more bleak than ever.

Just reaching adolescence, Eva is described as being, at this time, 'a small but buxom girl, brown-eyed and with dark brown, tousled hair'. She is also described as 'vain and moody, much given to the reading of film magazines'. If her sisters had been known for their relative docility (being fatherless and rejected repeatedly as bastards, docility might indeed have come naturally to them), Eva and her brother Juan were to make up for it. In fact, Juan had become known as a 'lad of the village', or a bad boy (a reputation he would take with him into adulthood), and Eva, while charming when she had to be, could display a ferocious rage and wilful nature.

Certainly, at fifteen, she was determined to escape the dreary provincialism of Junin. Also, by this time, she was willing to use her body as the means of escape.

For an illegitimate teenager in Argentina, particularly an attractive, 'buxom' girl, life could not have been easy. Already what the Argentinians term a *resentida*, a resentful one, Eva was aware of the crushing limitations imposed upon women in this country of relentless male chauvinism. Her mother, now widowed, had been compelled to use at least one 'protector' and Eva would have been aware of the situation and, most likely, deeply resentful of it. Now spending her days in the boarding house, surrounded by macho males, fetching, carrying, dusting, scrubbing and fighting off the inevitable advances of the boarders, she must have realised that her only hope of escape lay in the desires of such men. It was the men who had the freedom and earned the money to use it. And it was the men from Buenos Aires who could offer her the means of escape.

The vanity of the Argentinian male was such that he would sacrifice a great deal to have a young mistress who could pleasure him without making him feel that he was committed. However, the majority of such men, though proud to boast about their *casa chica*, felt only contempt for any *casa chica* not their own. It was into the steamy waters of this ripe hypocrisy that Eva would have to leap if she was to find an escape from dreary Junin – and she was able to make that leap because her growing contempt for men in general was her psychological protection.

Little is known about Eva at the time she first met the professional guitar-player and tango singer Agustin Magaldi, and it is possible that her subsequent liaison with him, at the tender of age of fifteen, was her first sexual experience. It is, however, likely that she had already dipped her toe into these dangerous waters in Junin itself, learning, as she would have done, that an unattached girl must make herself of some use to men if she is to gain anything remotely worth having. Certainly, in the enforced intimacy of a boarding house for males, she would not have been able to avoid the more obvious manifestations of her sexual allure to the men she was servicing as a maid.

She was 'buxom' and 'vain'. She would, therefore, have attracted the men and, given her vanity, taken a certain amount of pleasure from their attentions. However, she was not dealing with the kind of men she had read about in her movie magazines and secretly yearned to meet – the famous, the glamorous, the rich. Rather, she was in a boarding house that catered to passing trade and those men would have been low on the ladder: travelling salesmen, small farmers, lonely soldiers on leave, poor, frustrated bachelors living out of suitcases. Cleaning up after them, seeing their sperm on the bedsheets and their shit in the toilet bowls, learning of their secret vices and base desires and pathetic needs, would in no way have enhanced her affection for them. On the other hand, given her vanity and the growing awareness of her sexual power, it is safe to assume that overtures were made and, eventually, accepted.

What we *do* know is that she desperately wanted out and understood that she couldn't escape without the help of a man who had an interest in her. Also, aware that two of her sisters had been married off to lodgers and that her mother now wanted her to stay in Junin and run the boarding house, hopefully to marry a lodger and settle down in Junin, Eva must have been filled with despair and, perhaps, growing panic.

It is therefore not surprising that in 1934, when she was fifteen and saw Agustin Magaldi, at least ten years older than her, but a professional nightclub performer, handsome and debonair in his flashy suit and bow-tie, playing his guitar and singing in a nightclub in Junin, she was overwhelmed by his glamour – her first 'celebrity', after all – or, when she saw his interest in her, cold-bloodedly used it to her advantage.

Either way, she certainly met Magaldi after that first show, embarked on an affair with him, and eventually made her escape from Junin with him, adopting him as her 'protector' and guiding light. Whether she was victim or exploiter, it is a tribute to Eva's iron will, to her already highly developed sense of survival, that at fifteen, still a raw and relatively ignorant country girl, she packed her bags, sneaked out of her mother's boarding house, and fled on the arms of her older lover, Agustin Magaldi, to seek a new life under the bright, bewitching lights of Buenos Aires.

Chapter Five

Buenos Aires, the capital of Argentina, is the fifth biggest city in the world with flea markets, jockey clubs, polo clubs, nightclubs, cinemas and numerous theatres. French is the second language. In the 1930s, the wealthy sent their children to Paris or London to be educated. They also emulated the leisured, affected, luxurious lifestyle of Europe in the 1920s and, convinced that the wealth of the pampas would never dry up, were the biggest spenders in the days of big spenders.

While the beef and corn were shipped out of the magnificent harbour, making many Argentinians millionaires, the city also attracted the poor, who flooded in to search for work. As the city became more industrialised, so the demand for labourers was growing. The needs of industry were drawing the workers from the land, but these workers did not share in the wealth they produced. Thus, within this city of extravagant living and glamour, there were thousands who existed in dire poverty.

'On arriving there,' Eva says, 'I discovered it was nothing like I had imagined. On the outskirts I saw the deprived areas, and looking at the streets and houses, I realised that rich and poor did exist in the cities too . . . I have only experienced sadness that matched this disillusion on one other occasion in my life; that was when I discovered that the Three Wise Men didn't really come on their camels bearing gifts.'

It is hardly likely that at fifteen years of age, with the sophisticated Agustin Magaldi by her side, Eva would have shown concerns that were so altruistic. If disillusionment there was, it would have been of a more personal kind, based on the harsh realities of personal survival. She had just fled her home, she was living with an older man, a professional singer, and having already acted in a school play, *Arriba Estudiante* (*Students Arise*) and been stirred by the experience, she was determined to find fame as a star. Given this, her obsessions would not have been about the inequalities between rich and poor, but about how to find success and security for herself.

Though often described as buxom, Eva, with her peasant girl's speech, her country girl's taste in clothes, and her heavy, adolescent calves and ankles, was not particularly striking when placed alongside the beauties of Buenos Aires. Nevertheless, she had indomitable courage, the faith of the desperate, and so she had publicity pictures taken and then did the rounds of the theatrical agencies along the Avenida Corrientes, the Shaftesbury Avenue, or Broadway, of Buenos Aires.

Eva's growing contempt for men would be fuelled by this experience. Already haunted by the memory of her mother's hard life (her humiliation as a *casa chica* on the ranch in Los Toldos, bearing Juan Duarte's five children, all out of wedlock, then suffering the contempt of his legal family and the other villagers), she would find that the journey recently embarked upon with Magaldi (he using her body; she using his connections; a rancid alliance growing ever more bitter) must continue if she was to climb the slippery slopes of Buenos Aires show business.

29

Although the city then had three film companies, thirty-five theatres, nine radio stations and a considerable number of independent producers, acting jobs were not easy to find. But, if things were hard, Eva was not about to be defeated and, well armed with Magaldi's list of names and personal introductions, as well as her iron determination to succeed, she went out to suffer what she would for what she wanted so badly.

'At first, when she started work, things were hard for her,' Erminda says. 'I missed her a lot. I used to tell her: "Come back, Eva, come back home." She used to say: "Listen, sister, I will come back when I have conquered Buenos Aires."'

Given the casual sexual blackmail rampant along the Avenida Corrientes, very few were the women who rose unscathed to success. Indeed, the 'casting couch', whether a myth or a reality in Hollywood, was almost a way of life in Buenos Aires show-business circles. Eva and others like her would have been faced with a simple choice: lie down on the casting couch or get out. Eva didn't get out. Once she had learned the rules, she simply dropped Magaldi and started moving up the ladder, through a succession of men, never looking back to count the cost.

Later, when she became Santa Evita, it was this part of her life that the aristocracy could neither forget nor forgive.

Nevertheless, it was the life she led then. For a number of years she wandered the streets of downtown Buenos Aires, haunting the theatres and offices of the big producers, making contacts where she could, being obliging when necessary, smiling readily when the call came, and generally doing what she felt she had to do, no matter how distasteful.

Eventually noted along the Avenida Corrientes for her provocative skin-tight dresses and insatiable ambition, she was also known, particularly in the old port area, Boca Gorda, where she lived for a while, as a girl with 'a tongue to skin a donkey'. Indeed, Boca Gorda was a rough, colourful breeding ground for the *chirripos*, the spivs who gathered together in the crowded, narrow streets, their trousers of 'special masculine cut', their eyes ogling the passing women, their sharp tongues slicing the air with a stream of bawdy invective. Against such tongues only a rapier could advance and Eva sharpened her tongue accordingly. She also learned to protect herself when travelling on the notorious Buenos Aires underground system, which holds the world record for male soliciting, and to handle herself well when riding on the equally notorious *colectivo* buses to and from the city centre.

Such an experience could only make her cosmopolitan. No longer the gauche country girl, now slim and long-legged and crafty, she was developing that hardness, that protective veneer, which was her only shield against the humiliations of her low station in life. Her brightly painted red lips, which would later glisten on posters and hoardings all over Argentina (thus giving rise to rumours of her artistry in fellatio), were finding their needed experience in these teeming, amoral streets.

Nevertheless, while Eva, during those early years, starved on occasion, she gradually picked up modelling work for fashion houses and hairdressers; gained small parts in sponsored radio plays put on by Radio Argentina and Radio El Mundo; and, more importantly, frequented such Buenos Aires nightclubs as the

Gong, the Golden Gate and the Embassy, where tenth-rate actresses like herself, apart from making useful contacts, could supplement their low wages by selling their sexual favours to wealthy men.

Eventually, through sheer hard grind and ruthless, amoral determination, she began to find better work. She did it mostly through men – it was men who ran the business – and, although she despised them for how they were using her, she was not known to have many women friends either, perhaps viewing other actresses as competition. (How ironic, therefore, that she would later defend women's rights with a genuine passion.) One female friend, however, was the popular comedy actress, Señora Pierina Dealessi, who gave Eva her first professional acting job on the stage.

'Here, in this little theatre, in 1935, a thin little girl came to see me. "I want to work," she said. "My name is Eva Duarte." So I gave her the opportunity . . . Eva worked for many seasons here with me. Later she left my theatre. She worked for other companies. She did radio, cinema, and lots of other things. Step by step, she kept progressing in her career. Then, later on, I used to see her and ask her: "Are you the same little girl I knew? From where did you get all that fire? All that strength?" She used to smile and kiss me. That's how she was.'

Sympathetic to the struggling Eva, Dealessi gave her a small part in *La Señora de Perez*, produced for the Comedia Theatre in 1935. A soon-forgotten domestic comedy, it starred Eva Franco, one of Argentina's most popular actresses, and the actor Pascual Pelliciota. Eva was soon having a professionally helpful affair with Pelliciota and, though *La Señora de Perez* ran only a few weeks, by July that year she was acting in another, *There's a World in Every Home*. By June 1936 she was touring with *The Mortal Kiss*, a play about 'the evils of sexual promiscuity'. Thereafter the promiscuous Eva took everything she could get.

It is difficult to say just how much she achieved through talent and how much on the casting couches or in the beds of her various 'protectors' – but most reports of the time suggest that she was dreadful as an actress, lacking warmth and emotion, though she was supremely good at persuading producers, all male, to give her opportunities. ('A very, very poor actress,' said Cesar Marino, head of production at Radio Argentina. Nevertheless, like other men who thought little of her talents, Marino was instrumental in finding her acting work.) As for the 'fire' that Señora Dealessi remarked upon, this was more the fire of brute ambition, of steely self-conviction, than any great blossoming of histrionic ability.

Indeed, Eva's entry into films came about when, in 1937, she was interviewed by the theatre and movie magazine, *Sintonia*, and instantly embarked on an affair with its owner, the former racing driver Emilio Kartulovic. Given good exposure by Kartulovic, she was soon acting in her first movie, *Seconds out of the Ring* (1938), and engaging in an affair with its star Pedro Quartucci. She followed it up with a string of other, equally mediocre movies, including *The Charge of the Brave* (1939), *The Unhappiest Man in Town* (1940) and *A Sweetheart in Trouble* (1941). In none of them did she show the slightest shred of talent.

One is an actress or one is not. Eva wanted to be an actress for all the wrong reasons: because actresses were 'stars', led glamorous lives, had money and were admired by the whole world. The true actress has to empty herself and reconstitute herself as someone else; but Eva Duarte, haunted by her impoverished past, motivated by resentment and the desperate need to be successful, no matter how she did it, could not possibly imagine being anyone else, let alone feel emotions not her own.

'She was terrible, cold as an iceberg,' said Pierina Dealessi, 'incapable of stirring an audience.'

To put it mildly, young Eva was a blank on the screen, and, although she picked up work, it was not for her talent. Thus, instead of glamour, she found only the hard, demeaning slog of a bit player who has to spread her legs in order to feature briefly in trash. In this sense, she did it all – frothy comedy, high drama, too many costume epics – and we see her in the stills as a dark-haired, reasonably pretty, anonymous face that will leave no deep imprint on the memory. Nevertheless, she continued to work and, to her family back in Junin, she must indeed have seemed like the glamorous star she had wanted to be.

Still envious of her sister Blanca's blonde hair and, also, because she revered American movie actresses like Lana Turner, to whom she bore a passing resemblance, she dyed her dark hair blonde and moved closer to what she wanted to be: a wet dream for the masses.

Certainly it helped. By the time she had made *Le Cabalgata del Circo* (1944), her photograph was featured on the advertising poster and she was eighth on the cast list. She was blonde and bare-shouldered.

Nevertheless, she was hardly the 'star' she had wanted to be and she must have suffered her fair share of humiliations, sexual and otherwise, to get where she was. She despised these movies and the men who had put her in them, but she continued to be an actress while scheming to go on to bigger things and become her own woman. She didn't know quite how she would do it, but she was ready for anything.

In the event, it was two members of her family who led her onto the right road.

Eva's brother, Juan Duarte, was working in a bank in Buenos Aires and already gaining a reputation as someone with few scruples. (He was soon sacked for stealing money from the bank.) Handsome and dissolute, enjoying women and the night life, he mixed with a lot of people, some with dubious reputations, and had many valuable contacts in show business. After introducing Eva to a soap manufacturer who sponsored radio shows, he stood aside while Eva courted the man and seduced him into giving her work on Radio Belgrano, mainly in sponsored, weepy soap operas. Given regular employment and paid 150 pesos per month, Eva was soon renting an apartment in a more fashionable section of the city and, combining her radio work with the movies and bit parts in stage comedies, she started living a relatively good life. Since as an actress she was shallow, whereas her voice had its own resonance, eventually she was given her own radio slot, delivering gossipy news.

The second family member to help was Eva's sister, Elisa, who often visited with her husband, Major Alfredo Arrieta. It was through Arrieta that Eva met other army officers, notably a Colonel Anibal Imbert who, as Government Director of Posts and Telegraphs, was coaxed into helping her move higher up the ladder by forcing Radio Belgrano to pay her more money and give her more air space. Before long she was better known as a radio celebrity than she was as an actress.

Eva's relationship with Colonel Imbert was her first step on the road to a fame far beyond that of show business – and almost certainly, by this time, she was astute enough to know just what she was doing. While Argentina was then being run by a conservative coalition headed by president Ramón S. Castillo, the government was strongly – some would say almost totally – supported by the military. Army officers of senior rank were therefore men of enormous influence and authority. Introduced to such men by her brother-in-law, Major Arrieta, Eva saw how they could help her and, in particular, how Colonel Imbert, who as Director of Posts and Telegraph had such a strong influence on radio broadcasting, could advance her career. For this reason, Colonel Imbert became the first, though certainly not the last, of the many military officers who would be used and then cast aside by her as she moved up the ladder.

There can be no question that Eva was, at this time, using men in a cold-blooded pursuit of her goals. It is very likely that from the moment of her seduction by, or of, Agustin Magaldi, she had started to view her relationships with men as purely functional. They wanted her body and she needed their connections; each was therefore using the other in a bloodless transaction.

Eva managed to use her woman's wiles to open many doors, even though there was a coldness to her beauty. It was the kind that promises everything but real affection or warmth: a carefully made-up, alabaster, photogenic prettiness that goes no deeper than the paper on which it is printed. Nevertheless, her painted lips spoke to many of the whore's expertise at fellatio, her brown eyes had learned to flash with a feigned sensuality, and her body, now slimmed down by constant, ruthless dieting, was seductive in its tight-fitting clothes. She had long legs and showed them off.

She was, however, always working. She had the soul of a model so divorced from her own body that she can view it as no more than a tool, to be temporarily lent out and then reclaimed. Thus, there was a hard and calculating sheen to her beauty. It was all in the make-up, in the delicacy of her bone structure; it was not a beauty that sprang from within to capture the heart. Just as, much later, Evita would learn to change her appearance to suit the occasion (either modelled on a specific movie actress or on a famous historical figure) so, now, she was learning to split her personality and offer the separate pieces to her own advantage. Certainly there is little evidence that she ever had a relationship with a man who could not advance her career.

'Todos me acosan sexualmente,' she is quoted as saying of her actress days. 'Everybody makes a pass at me.'

Naturally they did. But if it is in the nature of the Latin-American male to make a pass at a woman like Eva, it was certainly in Eva's nature to respond to such a gesture only if the propositioning male was of some use to her.

The rumours (or truths) of Evita's history as a 'little whore', as an artiste in fellatio, would spring directly out of the national memory of Eva's early struggles in Buenos Aires. Argentinians love rumours. They also love the knowledge that all rumours are based on facts and that in this case the facts spoke for themselves. Eva was not a professional prostitute. She simply used what she possessed. She used it with men she had secretly come to despise and, in doing so, she had to despise herself.

Not for nothing would she, much later, when broadcasting as 'Santa Evita' from her sickbed, open up with the sublime Freudian slip: 'Ladies of Argentina, I am speaking to you from my old workbench!' If the dying Evita had been oblivious of her own remark, nevertheless it had sprung out of genuine recollections of her early, hard years in Buenos Aires. Eva's bed in Buenos Aires was the 'workbench' on which her future was shaped.

Giving herself to those men, who by the nature of the transaction would treat her contemptuously, Eva came to despise them (and their wealth and their power) and withdrew into a deeper, more feverish self where dreams of conquest and vengeance could sustain her.

As we have seen, her cultivation of members of the military sprang from her awareness that the ruling junta would always have a great deal of sway over broadcasting. And, just as she had taken up with Colonel Imbert in order to further her broadcasting career and exact larger wages from Radio Belgrano, so now she was about to drop Imbert and move on to the higher echelons of the most recent regime.

Argentine politics, which had, after the military coup of 1932, settled down into a vague form of democracy, were again being torn apart by conflicting ideologies. Indeed, after Pearl Harbor, the turmoil inside Argentina had been such that President Ramón Castillo was forced to proclaim a state of siege. This had come about because the government was split between the pro-Axis Argentine Army and his own conservative coalition, which believed in an Allied victory and so wanted to side with the Allies. The army generals, who favoured Hitler and Mussolini and were fed up with the vacillating policy of Castillo, had decided to make up his mind for him.

Thus, on 4 June 1943, General Arturo Rawson, Commander of the Cavalry School, led the small garrison down from the Campo Mayo and along the Avenida of the same name. Before they completed their march to Government House, President Castillo fled to a waiting gunboat on the River Plata. Consequently, General Rawson, who had merely carried out the plans of the Group of United Officers (GOU), announced from the balcony of the Casa Rosada the 'resignation' of President Castillo and the appointment of himself as Chief Executive.

The GOU, however, had other ideas and, after two days as President, General Rawson was forced to stand down and was sent off as Ambassador to Brazil. General Pedro Ramirez, the War Minister, was proclaimed as the new President, with a certain Colonel Juan Perón named as Secretary of Labour and Social Welfare.

In fact, Juan Perón was the real architect of the Revolution of June the Fourth – and his revolutionary ambitions were not yet quenched.

At this time, Eva Duarte was still working at Radio Belgrano (for something considerably more than 150 pesos per month) and, conscious that the ladder to success might be compounded of the military junta's mattresses, she kept her attention focused in that direction. Already notorious for her flamboyant attempts to bring herself to the notice of producers and other influential people (and consistently rejected by Hollywood, for which she despised the Americans), she now surprised even those closest to her with a piece of steely-nerved histrionics.

One night in July 1943, a month after the revolution, Eva went to a telephone in a room in Radio Belgrano and, turning to an actress friend, told her to listen. Picking up the phone, she dialled a number, announced herself as Eva Duarte of Radio Belgrano, and asked to speak to President Ramirez. Obviously enamoured by a call from the charming and popular radio actress, Ramirez decided to speak to her.

'Is that you, Pedro?' Eva said chirpily. 'This is Eva speaking. Yes, I'll be delighted to have dinner with you. Tomorrow evening. *Buenos*.'

The insolence – and the success – of this gesture soon reached the ears of Señor Jaime Yankelevich, the owner of Radio Belgrano. Though despising Eva as a pushy woman and rank opportunist, he was not a man to miss an opportunity when he saw one and so he promptly raised her salary to 5,000 pesos per month and gave her her own radio show.

Eva went on to have her dinner with President Ramirez and became his 'close friend', but eventually, on the advice of Señor Yankelevich, she turned her attention to one Colonel Guilbert, another of the leading revolutionaries whom Yankelevich felt would soon be of even more importance than Ramirez. A few months later, towards the end of 1943, on the set of her latest movie, *La Prodiga*, Eva was introduced by Colonel Guilbert to Colonel Juan Domingo Perón.

By now Eva had the well-earned reputation of being able to spot, and catch, the coming men; her choice, therefore, of Colonel Perón as a suitable target for her attentions (against the advice of Señor Yankelevich, who would later have cause to regret that he had been wrong) would suggest that she knew of Perón's activities in the new government and was aware that he would soon be going places. Subsequently, she discarded Colonel Guilbert and turned her inviting gaze upon Colonel Perón, a 48-year-old widower with a reputation for political ruthlessness and a passion for younger ladies, especially attractive actresses.

Eva Duarte, a well-known actress and radio personality, was twenty-four years old.

Chapter Six

Like Eva Duarte, Juan Domingo Perón was born in the pampas in the province of Buenos Aires. Also, like Eva, he was not one of the aristocratic *estanciero* (big rancher) class. A Creole, he was a descendant of families that had settled in Argentina for years, but he also had Italian and French ancestors, as do most Argentines in this land filled with immigrants. His grandfather was Dr Thomas Perón, a general practitioner greatly respected and well known in his district, but his father, Mario Perón, just like Eva's father, had no gifts or ambitions and worked on the ranch of the Guerrero family for many years. There he met and married a *chinita* (a country girl with Indian blood in her veins) working on the *estancia*.

Juan Domingo Perón was born on 8 October 1895, in the town of Lobos, sixty-five miles south of Buenos Aires. When he was five years old the family moved to Patagonia in the south, a desolate, cold, windswept terrain where, as he grew up, he was forced to live like a gaucho, learning to ride almost before he could walk, breaking wild horses, lassoing ostriches and eventually riding the stony, freezing *mesa*, wrapped only in a poncho and with silver spurs strapped to his bare feet. Like many upwardly mobile, lower-class, male youth, he entered the Army Military Academy in Buenos Aires in 1911, at sixteen years of age, became a sub-lieutenant two years later, and was promoted to a full lieutenant at twenty. A fine athlete, muscular and full of energy, he distinguished himself in boxing, fencing, marksmanship and skiing, as well as excelling at German, Italian and, to a lesser degree, English. At a relatively young age he married Aurelia Tisson, a schoolteacher of French descent, and was presented with a daughter, Maria Inez. There would be no further children and his wife would die (like Evita, of cancer) in 1938, rarely to be mentioned again.

Perón was often to say that his great-grandfather was a Sardinian senator; and, while this may or may not have been true, he could have been Italian on his father's side, as a few of the older residents of Lobos recalled a time when the Peróns were called Peroni. Since, on his mother's side, there was supposed to be Argentine Indian blood, the full-grown Perón could well have been of unusual character. Certainly the Italian side of Perón had always been evident in his grandiloquent gestures, his hearty (and frequently false) laughter, and his tendency to greet and leave friends with a crushing *abrazo*, or embrace.

If this more public side of Perón was evidence of his Italian descent, his more private nature, which was in fact humourless, might have sprung from the pragmatism of his French blood. However, Perón was harder than that. Like Eva Duarte, he was impelled by the need for domination and absolute devotion from those around him. He also possessed a total ruthlessness and lack of morality when pursuing his goals.

Noted at both school and the Army Military Academy more for his brawn than for his brains, he was frequently involved in brawls because of his inflammable temper. That he rarely lost such fights might be due to the fact that he rarely fought only with his fists, but instead would throw anything that came

43

to hand before closing in on his victim with terrifying ferocity. Although, as with his schooldays, he did not distinguish himself as a scholar, he *was* distinguished by his Latin-American good looks, by his 'film star' smile, and by the fact that for a number of years he held the Army Swordsmanship Championship and was always in the top bracket of expert riflemen.

After being promoted to full lieutenant, he was assigned to the General Arenales Infantry Regiment. Two years after his unremarkable period as an infantry officer, he received an appointment to the General Staff. The following year, he was transferred to the Ministry of War as Private Secretary to the Minister, but, when the Minister became dissatisfied with his performance in this undemanding position, he was appointed Professor of Military History at the Senior School of War (*Escuela Superior de Guerra*). After five years as a captain, he received a routine promotion to major.

Though Perón prided himself on his macho image, there was a slight feminine streak to his make-up. This had been noticed at the Army Military Academy and was also noticed at the Senior School of War. His feminine streak took the form of a certain childishness, a girlish petulance when things went wrong, and a distinct, overweening vanity. Later there would be widely circulated stories about Perón's extracurricular activities with both young girls *and* young boys, but there is no record of any particular incidents at the Military Academy beyond the fact that he was a womaniser with a particular fondness for 'very young girls'. Given his dashing good looks and his total lack of morality, it is safe to assume that he rarely suffered a lack of young girls.

In 1930, at the age of thirty-five, he took part in the military revolution led by General Jose E. Uriburu, an event now seen by many as the first step on the downhill path of Perónism. Returning to his duties at the Senior School of War, he wrote several books on military strategy in which his admiration for Hannibal, Julius Caesar and Napoleon was clearly evident. Intent on paying tribute to the genius of German military might, he plagiarised Clausewitz, blamed the loss of the First World War on the ABC Conference (Argentina, Brazil and Chile, 1916) and assured his readers that, the next time around, the Big Three would agree and move together against the Allies. Because of this, he was recommended to the Nazi government as Argentina's coming man.

Perón's ability to bend with the prevailing wind was most evident in his complicity with the Nazis. In 1938, when Hitler was sending vast sums of money to Argentina to suborn the notoriously hard-up officers of the Argentine Army into sympathy with the Third Reich, Juan Perón, now promoted to lieutenant-colonel, was appointed Military Attaché on the staff of the Argentine Embassy in Chile – one of the two countries (the other was Uruguay) strongly opposed to Hitler's proposed *Bloque Austral*. Shortly after arriving to take up his position in the Embassy, Perón was accused by the Chilean government of being the head of an espionage ring backed by the Nazis.

Added to this indictment was a protest at his conduct with teenagers of both sexes.

Displeased with Perón's bungling, the Nazis promptly disowned him. He was, however, reinstated in their good books when he cultivated the friendship of General Freidrichs Wolf, the Nazi agent, and became infamous for the golden handshakes he received for his protection of many other Nazis. Eventually he solicited Mussolini (whom he revered) and had himself appointed Military Attaché to the Argentine Embassy in Rome. While there, he never missed a speech by Mussolini, closely studied his style of oratory, and adapted it for his own future use. He also studied the way in which Mussolini controlled all of Italy from Rome and he resolved to do the same in Argentina.

When not engaged in these more serious matters, Perón picked up a reputation as an insatiable party-goer, embarked on a brief but intensive tour of the other dictator-controlled countries such as Germany, Hungary, Albania, Spain and Portugal, and dallied with playful Nazis in Paris. It was in Paris, in 1939, that gossiping French tongues spread the news that Juan Domingo Perón shared with the Nazis certain aberrations of a kind not strictly political.

Still ambitious and still committed to the army, he was placed in charge of troops in Mendoza in 1941 and started a 'crusade of spiritual renovation', which worked out as a scheme to staff the Argentine government with idealistic, hard-working and deeply nationalistic young army officers. This idea crystallised into the GOU, an organisation of officers below the rank of general. The letters stood for *Grupo de Oficiales Unidos* (Group of United Officers) and were later idealised into *Gobierno, Orden, Unidad* (Government, Order, Unity).

Back in Argentina, Perón formed his GOU by using blackmail to force the resignations of those officers who dared to disagree with him. Since most of these officers had borrowed money from the German bank in Buenos Aires, when Hitler was generously buying their support, Perón, who was in possession of the recorded transactions of all those who had made withdrawals, had no problem in either enlisting them or getting them to sign their resignation papers.

In 1943, the GOU, of which Perón was now the acknowledged head, launched the Revolution of June the Fourth, which sent the unpopular President Ramón Castillo running for the gunboat on the River Plata and briefly installed General Arturo Rawson as President. Two days later, General Rawson was replaced by General Pedro P. Ramirez and Perón, after a brief period as Secretary of Labour and Social Welfare, became Vice-President and Minister of War.

Thus, by the time Perón met Eva Duarte for the first time, ironically on the set of her movie, *La Prodiga*, his acceptance of corrupt methods to obtain his own ends was an ineradicable part of his nature.

The future *Patron* and the future *Santa* Evita held hands.

Chapter Seven

A week after their first meeting, Eva Duarte and Colonel Perón were to be seen wining and dining at El Tigre, a riverside resort of shaded creeks and restaurants just outside Buenos Aires. Within days of this meeting, Eva began arriving at Radio Belgrano in a War Ministry car and her salary soon spiralled accordingly. Rumours then spread that Eva had marched around to Perón's apartment in the Calle Posadas and thrown out his teenage mistress. Whether or not this was true, Eva certainly moved into the apartment directly adjoining Perón's and was soon spending as much time in his apartment as she was in her own.

News of the liaison spread like wildfire through the streets of Buenos Aires and was soon filling newspapers nationwide. If other members of the military junta were quietly uneasy about the relationship – aware of Eva's reputation as a 'little whore' who had used other military officers to get where she was – the general public, particulary the 'shirtless ones', had no such qualms. In fact, they loved the idea of their beloved Eva Duarte, well-known radio commentator and minor movie actress, getting together with the flamboyant army colonel. Eva was tiny and Perón was tall; Eva was slim and Perón was broad – a veritable brute of a man – and many excited *descamisados*, in the bars and cafés, in the slaughterhouses and docks, bartered lewd jokes about how he and she, the long and the short of it, went about doing what they did when the lights were turned out.

'Put a bull onto a mouse,' they might say, 'and what's left on the bedsheets?'

They did it, in particular, because of Eva's reputation – her colourful days in Boca Gorda, the rumours of expertise in fellatio, the many men who had been and gone, including other military officers – and they did it possibly because they had wet dreams about her and envied Perón. But the 'shirtless ones' admired Perón just as they fantasised about Eva: he was a true Argentinian, a real macho man, while she was a poor girl who had fought her way up from the pampas to become a successful, glamorous creature who could mix with the likes of him. So the 'shirtless ones' followed the affair with great interest and discussed it endlessly.

Within weeks, the relationship between Eva and Perón, played out boldly before the public, had turned Eva, once a minor celebrity, into an object of feverish speculation – a star in her own right.

Now she was under the patronage of her new 'protector', Colonel Juan Perón, the politically powerful Secretary of Labour and Social Welfare, Eva's career suddenly climbed to dizzying heights. Described by most drama critics as a 'cold' and 'unexpressive' actress, she nevertheless found herself in as many movies as she wanted and with an authority that was irresistible to her. ('We had to put up with her domineering everybody,' said Juan Jose Miguez, the nominal star of *Spendthrift*.) Already beginning to live out her grandiose fantasies, she was soon interviewing leading members of the junta for her radio programmes and being photographed with them in the

Radio Belgrano studios and on her film sets. Before long, she had persuaded, or bullied, Señor Yankelevich (who now dreaded the sight of her) into letting her star in a series of plays inspired by the lives of great women, including Catherine the Great, Lady Hamilton, Queen Elizabeth I, Madame Chiang Kai-shek, and so forth. In none of these roles did Eva show signs of greatness. However, the Radio Association of Argentina was founded during this period and Eva, to no one's surprise, was nominated as President.

There were many in those days who saw Eva's affair with the much older Perón as no more than a 'little whore's' bid for the pot of gold. Certainly there could be no doubt that Perón was infatuated with her (he had always chased actresses, particularly *young* actresses, and Eva was precisely half his age), but whether or not this infatuation was returned in kind was the question that many asked themselves. Eva's reputation for deliberately pursuing influential men made many doubt the sincerity of her feelings for Perón. It was widely felt that she was using him, exploiting his infatuation with her, in order to further her career; and, since Eva had never had an affair with a man who could not help her, there were certainly strong grounds for so thinking.

Yet if Eva was not in love with Perón in the normal sense of the word, it is possible that she *was* infatuated with his unbridled ambition. Perón wanted to be President. He had *always* wanted to be President. He lived for the army and the army represented the country. Perón's ambitions knew no limits. He was totally fearless. Like Eva, he had a need to succeed that was almost abnormal.

It was possible that Evita could not truly love anyone – yet she *could* feel infatuation. She had been infatuated for years with her dreams of great achievement and Perón, in his own way, shared that dream. It is likely, therefore, that she became infatuated with him, or with what he represented, and was swept up, beyond love or even affection, into their binding relationship. Her own words, which cannot always be trusted, do at least suggest this.

We loved each other and we loved each other because we both had the same aim. In different ways, we both wanted to do the same thing; he, knowing exactly what he wanted to do, while I only felt it in my bones. He had intelligence; I had my heart. He was prepared for the struggle; I was ready for anything. But I knew nothing. He was educated and I was unsophisticated. He was huge and I was tiny. He was the teacher and I was the pupil. He was the figurehead and I was his shadow. He was sure of himself and I had extraordinary confidence in him.

Even propaganda has its buried truths. If not loving Perón in the normal sense of the word, Eva certainly loved what he represented and could offer to her. Her infatuation was therefore genuine. She was truly obsessed with Perón. He was educated and he would teach her; he was sophisticated and he would guide her; he had power and he would use it to unshackle her from all the old chains.

How could she not be infatuated? What other man could so clearly reflect her self-image? Perón was moved by ambitions beyond mere sex and other sen-

51

sual pleasures: like Eva, he had a larger role to play. His very presence made her think this. His restless energy gave her strength. Despised, humiliated, Eva had stored up her resentments and now believed in nothing but the will to succeed. To succeed, one must fight. Not to succeed was unthinkable. There were only the rulers and the ruled and she could not be the latter.

Eva saw life in those terms. Creativity was conquest. She could not love the poor, but she could certainly hate the rich, and she confused the one emotion with the other. Confusing her contempt for the rich with her sympathy for the poor, she felt a great spiritual awakening that would not be diminished.

Eva and Juan Perón complemented each other. He wanted power and she would guide him to its source and capturing it would weld them together. Yes, Eva loved Perón. Her fevered emotions told her that. She would be but his shadow, she would encourage his every step, and she would nudge him to the fountainhead of power, where he might then unveil her and show her the world. She in turn would gain everything.

Eva knew where the power lay. It lay with the workers, the *descamisados*, the 'shirtless ones', who had been sleeping for centuries.

While Colonel Perón, as the publicly known Secretary of Labour and Social Welfare and the shadowy head of the GOU, was surreptitiously juggling assignments and slipping his own men into all the important government posts, he was also quietly adding to his duties the Directorship of the National Labour Department and loudly persuading the more timid

President Ramirez to elevate that same department into a Secretariat of Labour and Welfare, which would make it much more powerful, with himself as Director. By November 1943 he had succeeded.

By now, Perón was coming under harsh criticism from the press, the universities and the Labour movement. He had not previously thought of the potential in organised labour support and it is likely that he first started thinking about it after his girlfriend, Eva Duarte, in one of her on-the-spot broadcasts from a riverside slum, gave a gushing eulogy to 'this new genius [Perón] who will become a father to our poor.' Certainly it was shortly after this that the lawyer, Juan Atilio Bramuglia, a great friend of Eva's and barrister to the Union of Railwaymen, joined the Perón gang and persuaded the railwaymen, who had the strongest and best-organised trade union in the country, to become the first Labour supporters of the future dictator.

Subsequently, on 27 November 1943, Perón officially opened his Secretariat of Labour and Welfare with an impassioned and (for him) unexpected support for the suppressed *descamisados*.

There can be little doubt that the driving force behind this sudden love of the 'shirtless ones' was Eva Duarte. Now a celebrity in her own right, but despised by the snobbish middle classes of Buenos Aires as a 'little whore' who had found success on her back, on the 'workbench' of her bed – obsessed also with her past, her memories of poverty and humiliation – Eva genuinely saw the workers as her (and the country's) salvation. If Perón, on the other hand, had rarely thought of the workers, but had instead cherished his belief in the purity of the army, he was now listening more and more to the public broadcasts and the private conversations of his mistress.

Eva used this brilliantly. Aware of the slumbering power of the workers, she was now specialising in a brand of propaganda, put out over the radio, that heaped vilification on the ruling classes and espoused Perón as the saviour of the country.

Because of this, and particularly after Perón's cunning November speech, when he had formally opened his Secretariat of Labour and Welfare, President Ramirez was growing worried. Having foolishly gone on holiday over the Christmas period, he sent an order forbidding Perón to make any more public speeches without permission, then he, President Ramirez, hurried back to Buenos Aires.

He was too late. A devastating earthquake had hit San Juan and Perón, as head of the new Secretariat of Labour and Welfare, hurried to the scene of the disaster, where he organised a San Juan Relief Fund of £4 million and drenched the country with so many heartrending speeches that he became, virtually overnight, a national figure, hailed as the 'Saviour of San Juan'. This event was also publicised by Eva Duarte on her evening radio programmes (during which she repeatedly mentioned 'the handsome colonel' and 'his good deeds') and was puffed up even more when, in Buenos Aires' Luna Park, the Actors' Association organised a benefit festival in aid of the victims. It was midway through this festival that Colonel Perón and Eva Duarte were 'formally' introduced – and this very public occasion not only cemented Perón's popularity with the *descamisados* but also marked the start of the 'official' relationship between Perón and Eva.

(No satisfactory account was ever made of the disposal of the £4 million San Juan Relief Fund contributions. With the earthquake quickly forgotten, only the survivors were to know that little more than a token reconstruction of San Juan had been undertaken and that even this was subsequently dropped. Shortly after, Perón supervised and financed the construction of a special 'home' for a number of 'attractive' teenage orphans. It was widely believed that he did so with the money originally donated for the reconstruction of San Juan.)

Events now progressed with bewildering speed. All too aware of Perón's popularity with the *descamisados* and of his intention to eventually become President himself, President Ramirez ordered a thorough investigation of the Ministry of War and the Secretariat of Labour and Welfare. When the investigation revealed that all the major posts in the Ministry were held by Perón's GOU officers, Ramirez, on 23 February 1944, declared the GOU formally dissolved and then called for Perón's resignation.

That night, six of Perón's GOU officers walked into Ramirez's study and forced him, at gunpoint, to sign his own resignation. By the following morning a new government had been formed, officially headed by Ramirez's Vice-President, General Edelmiro Farrell. Since everyone knew that Farrell was no more than Perón's trained seal, there could be little doubt in anyone's mind as to who held the real power. By 4 May, Perón was Minister of War and by 7 July he was the Vice-President of Argentina.

Eva Duarte was now showing her fangs – both as a revered public figure and as a private, vindictive

55

woman. In June, even America's *Time* magazine (which Eva would eventually ban in Argentina) was reporting: 'The breathless eight-month rise of Eva Duarte from artistic obscurity to one of Argentina's highest-paid radio contracts is the talk of Buenos Aires. Eva is lovely to look at – tall, svelte, brunette, alabaster-skinned, twenty-six. She is also the favourite of Colonel Juan Perón, Minister of War and strong-boy of Argentina.'

Time had never been renowned for the accuracy of its columns and its report was inaccurate on a few counts. Eva, if a natural brunette, was then blonde. She was not 'tall' but was actually only 5ft 2in, a sly deception being practised by the use of her three-inch heels. However, *Time* then recounted a story that was in essence true.

Eva, now known by the diminutive of 'Evita' (little Eva), was in competition with Nina Cascallar, the then favourite of Captain Villegas, Argentine Federal Interventor of National Radios. The confrontation between Eva and Nina occurred on one of Argentina's national holidays when Radio Belgrano, Buenos Aires' most popular broadcasting station, fell behind schedule. Nina, who was supposed to go on the air ten minutes before Evita, wanted to be heard, although her time had already overlapped with Evita's. Evita refused to give her the extra time and, being the mistress of Colonel Perón, received official backing from a Belgrano official.

Stung, Nina waited until Colonel Perón left town the following week for an inspection trip to Cordoba Province. Then, one night during that week, just before Evita was scheduled to go on the air as star of *My Kingdom for Love*, a version of the Elizabeth

Essex romance, someone in the control room switched on the microphone prematurely and listeners all over Argentina heard the announcer exclaiming, 'That tart is on!'

The Press-Propaganda Office promptly hit Radio Belgrano with a forty-eight-hour advertising suspension for 'expressions which constituted an affront to the nation's culture and violated the fundamental principles of broadcasting, which today is the greatest vehicle for the diffusion of spiritual, social and moral culture.' By the time the suspension was lifted, it had cost Radio Belgrano £2,000 worth of advertising revenue – and it also cost Nina Cascallar her job.

The affront had not been to the nation's culture, but to the mistress of the Minister of War, Colonel Juan Perón.

And Evita was now Radio Belgrano's leading lady.

With Evita now in a position to become the most powerful propagandist in the country, and with Perón established as official Vice-President and unofficial leader of Argentina, the great love spectacle of the century could begin.

Chapter Eight

Perón and Evita now set out to build an unbreakable political power structure. Since successive governments had ignored the country's underpaid labourers, the *descamisados*, Perón began his bid for the Presidency by announcing that he was a 'syndicalist', a 'patriot' and 'the first Argentine worker'. In fact, even as he was publicly aligning himself with the 'shirtless ones', he was quietly incarcerating the labour leaders who had turned against him in prison camps in El Chaco and Patagonia. This task completed, he took control of the unions by seducing their remaining leaders with highly paid government jobs.

Urged on by Evita, now the secret fantasy mistress of the working masses, he began talking the language of the workers; was photographed sharing wine with them in waterfront bars, dressed as casually as they were; pretended to listen to, and take note of, their grievances; and finally, having already bought off their remaining leaders (those more easily corrupted than the ones he'd thrown into prison), he installed his own supporters as the new heads of the unions. Also, more often than not in the company of the glamorous and increasingly popular Evita, he began personally attending innumerable labour meetings up and down the country. Together, he and Evita sought out the workers in the shanty towns of Buenos Aires, in the slaughterhouses of Avellaneda, the granary centres of Rosario and Santa Fé, the industrial cities of Cordoba, the vineyards of Mendoza, even the remote rural regions of Salta and Corrientes, in order to win their hearts and minds.

Adopting the style of oratory he had learned from his hero, Mussolini, Perón became increasingly successful at convincing the *descamisados* of his sincerity in wishing to place the country's affairs in their hands. In this he was helped enormously by Evita who, having become the most popular woman in the country, their very own 'little Eva', would give lengthy speeches in her impassioned, actressy manner: voice raging, brown eyes blazing, hands waving expressively above her blonde head, spine curved, breasts out-thrust, her crimson lips pouting and beseeching, reminding them of where she had come from and what she was supposed to be good at: her carnal road to sainthood. Evita was saint and sinner to them, and they could not resist her.

In fact, Evita now believed in her own manifest destiny. Having literally turned herself into one of her imaginary childhood heroines, she was living the role to the hilt and being raised on high by it. At last she had a reason to be and it was greater than she was. Already a celebrity, the focus of mass dreams (star of stage, screen and radio; her picture on the cover of newspapers and magazines), she now viewed her growing legion of fans, the *descamisados*, as extensions of herself. A poor girl from the pampas, exploited and abused, she knew exactly how the workers suffered and felt at one with them. She knew what they needed, what they wanted, and she shared their frustration. They in turn were the heart and soul of the country and she could unite them.

Driven by a huge ego and supremely self-dramatising, Evita came to believe the very myth she was creating about herself, now seeing her past struggles and countless humiliations as the fire in which her destiny had been forged.

'I'm not leading my people because destiny demands it,' she would say later, 'but because, perhaps without realising it, I prepared myself as if I knew instinctively that one day this responsibility and privilege would fall to me.'

Evita created her own legend. Having created it, she then came to believe it and felt herself sanctified.

The combination of sex and sincerity was irresistible to the masses. For how many generations had the *descamisados* dreamed of attaining power, of tearing the wealth out of the hands of the bourgeoisie who had ruthlessly abused and exploited them? Now that power was being offered. Now that wealth would soon be theirs. Now the old, suppressive structure was being torn down to make way for self-rule and social justice. Even better, it was being offered by Juan Perón – not a remote politician, but a common man like themselves, a true child of the pampas, and a bold, macho soldier who (and how could they not admire this?) had an eye for the ladies.

And what a lady he now had! Their very own little Eva – Evita – this beauty who had escaped the same poverty that imprisoned them, who like them had suffered hardships and dreadful humiliations, who had offered her full, crimson lips and her 'little whore's' artistry as the price to be paid for her freedom.

How many of them had dreamed about her? How many had worshipped her on the screen? How many had thrilled to her voice on the radio, its histrionic sensuality, its promise of forbidden fruit, and imagined that she was talking personally to them?

Too many to count.

The whole show was irresistible: two children of the pampas, one of whom becomes a courageous military hero, the other his beautiful, blonde mistress, both of whom go on, hand in hand, to lead their people to glory. Love and sex and suffering and commitment – a soap opera for the long deprived, yearning masses; a fairy tale for the times.

To the average working Argentinian, who thrives on romance and scandal, the love affair between Juan Perón and little Eva was a blandishment beyond hope of resistance, an almost total seduction.

By the middle of 1945, Perón and Evita had a massively unionised country with the unions firmly under their control. Now heavily infiltrated by Perón's minions, the unions were faced with his Six-Point Labour Plan: (1) State control of all unions; (2) The State to elect the union members; (3) No central controlling union; (4) Suppression of political activities; (5) Submission to the judgement of the State in solving industrial problems; (6) Army discipline and military organisation methods for the unions. Thus backed by the growing authority of the State and reinforced with the allies he had built up within the unions, Perón now held a power much greater than the military itself could hope to command. National leadership was therefore his (and Evita's) next goal.

Though the Second World War was ending and Perón was being deprived of the support of the Nazis, it was becoming clear to one and all – particularly to the ruling classes and the students of the universities – that he was trying to set up a self-serving fascist dictatorship. In June 1945, the Socialist and Radical Parties violently expressed their antagonism to Perón's affairs and similar passions then raged throughout the whole of Argentina, with the students, in particular, demonstrating noisily and frequently. By August, an extraordinary anti-government coalition of conservatives, radicals, socialists and communists was demanding that the Supreme Court should take over the administration of the country and hold an election. By September, thousands of student protestors were marching through the streets of Buenos Aires.

Perón reacted by closing down the universities and sending most of their deans and rectors to jail. When the students counter-reacted by once more swarming into the streets, they were attacked by mounted police and armoured vehicles; others were fired upon by the army, resulting in many casualties; and thousands were arrested and imprisoned. Refusing to quit, the students barricaded themselves into the colleges and surrendered only when attacked with tear-gas bombs. By this time, the members of the coalition's Board of Democratic Coordination were either in prison or in hiding – and the beloved Evita, who had never shown fear before, was carrying a hand grenade for protection.

Stories of wholesale beatings and tortures were rife at this time and many of them were later substantiated.

By now, even the Argentine army was suffering dissension within its ranks and there were officers who, fearing that the increased public disorder would result in the overthrow of the entire social structure, felt that Perón must be restrained. This came to a head on 9 October, when senior officers of the Campo de

Mayo met in a council of war and decided that Perón had to go. Stung by this news, Perón, a mere Vice-President, sent his message boy, President Farrell, to the Campo de Mayo to slap the wrists of the recalcitrant officers. Farrell did not return. Instead, Generals Pistarina and von der Becke arrived with the statement: 'The President feels it is advisable that you should resign.' Left with no choice, Perón reluctantly signed his resignation papers.

By 12 October the whole of the government had resigned, with General Farrell remaining as President, though General Avalos was effectively in charge. That night, Perón was arrested, escorted on to the gunboat *Independencia*, and then transferred to prison on Martín García Island.

The Kingdom of Evita was at hand.

Chapter Nine

Evita had gained power by offering her love and was now hopelessly in love with power itself. Having seen the light of glory in the eyes of the *descamisados*, having captured them with her Goebbels-like mastery of the radio (her voice rising and falling, now murmuring, now shrieking, now emoting with a vibrant, sensual sob) she suddenly saw her chance to strike out on her own and align herself with Perón.

Whether or not Perón was in love with her or simply wanted her body, he was certainly now aware that their romantic–political relationship was one of his most potent weapons. It will never be known if he would have approved what she was planning; what is certain is that, once the plan had succeeded, he could not let her go for fear of losing the support of the *descamisados*. Yet he must have been worried. Who really controlled the *descamisados*? If they loved Evita more than they loved Perón, how much of his forthcoming power would he have to share with her?

Juan Perón sat in jail. Evita schemed to get him out. She had been attracted to Perón's power and his power was now growing every day. As a woman alone, Evita could not rule Argentina, but with Perón beside her, with her pulling the strings, she could exact vengeance for all the old wrongs and raise herself to unassailable heights. Given her subsequent actions and her fierce resentment of the Oligarchy, it would seem that the salvation of Perón was solely a political move.

While Perón was sweating it out in the island jail of Martín García, his friends in the unions organised a revolt of the workers on his behalf. Perón had gone to prison on 12 October. By 16 October the slaughteryard and packing-house workers of the nearby towns had begun to move into Buenos Aires by train, truck and foot. By the 17th, they had occupied the city. On that same day, Perón's strong-arm union man, Cipriano Reyes (who would later be brutally tortured in one of Perón's prisons), persuaded the factory owners that it would be 'healthy for themselves' if they closed down their factories for a day's holiday. Subsequently, that morning, thousands of workers poured across the Riachuelo Bridge to demonstrate in front of the Central Military Hospital where, so it had been rumoured, Colonel Perón was due to arrive for treatment.

This rumour was true in the sense that Perón had been complaining of pleurisy (a ruse to have himself removed from the island prison and thus, automatically, out of captivity), and that General Farrell, after seeing the thousands of workers in the capital, decided to capitulate and use Perón's hospitalisation as an excuse for releasing him.

As for Evita, who had been relentlessly stirring the masses with her histrionic radio speeches, she was also arranging for every kind of transport to bring loads of workers, male and female, from the neighbouring towns and villages. By late afternoon of 17 October, the centre of Buenos Aires was packed with thousands of workers, most of whom were coatless (a shocking sight in bourgeois Buenos Aires) and, even worse, shirtless.

It was then that Evita, shrieking passionately into a microphone placed high above the teeming thousands, turned the word '*descamisados*' – formerly a shameful term – into one of glorification and self-respect.

'This word *descamisados*,' she cried out, 'has been transformed into a synonym for struggle, for revindication, for justice, for truth! It has created a state of national conscience! It has been implanted in the soul of the people, like a magic impulse, to carry them forward!'

The thousands of *descamisados* roared their approval – and that roaring gradually changed into the thunderous, repetitive chanting of 'PAY-RÓN! PAY-RÓN! PAY-RÓN!' Given this, President Farrell had no choice but to give in. That evening, a car fetched Perón from the hospital and took him directly to the Casa Rosada (the Government House in the Plaza de Mayo from which many a President had previously fled) while the howling mobs raced around the vehicle. Amid scenes of mass hysteria, President Farrell, now repentant, and Colonel Perón, now forgiving, appeared together on the palace balcony and embraced. Colonel Perón then offered an impassioned speech in which he gave his 'first welcome' to the true soul of the country: namely, the roaring *descamisados*.

On 21 October 1945, Juan Domingo Perón and Maria Eva Duarte were married in a secret ceremony performed in her home town of Junin. The marriage was to be solemnised, on 10 December, with a church ceremony in the town of La Plata.

If love had formed part of the marriage, it had certainly not formed the whole. In fact, the marriage had sprung out of political motives. All of Buenos Aires and much of the rest of Argentina had been speculating on the next development in the Great Argentine Love Story. If Perón's *casa chica* was the collective dream of the *descamisados*, she could not be allowed to remain as such: Perón either had to get rid of her or legitimise the relationship. While many felt that Perón was reluctant to do either (he may have wanted Evita, but he was also wary of her), his closest friends and supporters felt that the popularity of his *casa chica* made it mandatory that their union should be legalised. Thus it was that Perón and Evita, the dream couple of Argentina, finally became man and wife.

Evita could now exact vengeance on all those who had wronged her.

First to feel the hand of retribution was Señor Yankelevich of Radio Belgrano. Long weary of the incessant demands of his influential minor actress, Yankelevich, upon hearing of the arrest of Juan Perón, had given Evita the boot. Ten days later, as Perón embraced President Farrell on the balcony of the Casa Rosada, Yankelevich not only had to let Evita resume her place behind the microphone but was forced to pay her for her absence, give her another enormous rise in salary, and throw in limitless freedom regarding the contents of her programme.

From this point on, Evita more or less ran Radio Belgrano.

Determined to be the First Lady of Argentina (having, as it were, already sampled the unique benefits of power), she used her control over Radio Belgrano to shower the listeners, in particular the *descamisados*, with her love and Perón's undying devotion. Given such sterling support, Perón launched himself forth as Presidential candidate, first resigning from the army, then proclaiming at a rally of his supporters: 'I join the ranks of the *descamisados*!'

To ensure that he would have the full support of the shirtless ones, he had the government decree that all employers must pay their workers a thirteenth month's wage as an annual bonus. Thus buying the loyalty of the formerly oppressed workers, he went on to suppress all opposition. With Evita on Radio Belgrano and with all other radio stations strictly controlled, his police and bully boys went out to break up all opposition meetings. The Oligarchy and the Jews soon became the common enemy, antagonistic foreign journalists were threatened and beaten up, and a lot of middle-class professional people had their collars and ties shorn off.

According to Spruille Braden, the then American Ambassador to Argentina, 'civil liberties, the right of assembly, and the freedom of both speech and the Press' were suspended. Braden also described the Presidential candidate as 'a self-styled Leader, supported by a Party aping its Nazi prototype'. Within days of this report, Peronist leaflets appeared in the streets of Buenos Aires, describing the American Ambassador as an 'undershirt diplomat', a 'cowboy', a 'rustler' and a 'gangster' comparable to Al Capone. Also, Braden's life was threatened.

The Peronist cause steamrollered on. In November, a new Labour Party made its appearance in Argentina, headed by Perón's old friends, Cipriano Reyes and Luis Gay. Included in their programme was the nationalisation of telephones, electric power and railways – all of which were predominantly owned by foreigners – and shorter hours and a share in the profits for industrial workers. After passionately proclaiming his faith in the New (Peronist) Argentina, Luis Gay, President of the new party, announced Colonel Juan Perón as his candidate for President.

In an attempt (ultimately successful) to gain the support of the strong Radical Party, Perón found ministerial posts in President Farrell's government for Juan Hortensio Quijano and a couple of his fellow deputies. Forming an organisation called the Radical Reconstruction Committee, the three collaborationists prepared for a Nomination Convention in the New Year to put forward Perón and Quijano as their candidates for President and Vice-President respectively. A few days later, the Labour Party nominee for the Vice-Presidency, Colonel Mercante, was forced to stand down and make way for Perón and Quijano.

The Peronists and trade unions now arranged a full-scale *blitzkrieg* against the opposition, breaking into their offices, disrupting their public meetings, beating up their supporters, and calling in both the federal police and the army when strong-arm tactics were required. Allied to this was an increasingly brutal campaign against the Jewish quarter ('Be a patriot: kill a Jew!' was an early slogan of the *Peronistas*) and the arrest of countless members of the Oligarchy, including 'ex-Foreign Ministers, Nobel prize-winners, surgeons and leading land-owners'. By December, Buenos Aires had become a battleground of street fights, riots, police baton charges, tear-gas attacks, shooting, bomb-throwing and arson, with crowds of frightened citizens fighting daily for places on board the steamers to Montevideo.

Appalled by what was going on, Argentina's few remaining independent businessmen arranged a lock-out early in the New Year as a protest. Known as the Employers' Strike, it was the most threatening opposition that Perón had had to face so far. He solved the problem by summoning the trade union leaders and pointing out to them that, if the employers held up production for a period of even a few months, the power of the Perónist movement might be smashed forever, leaving them back where they had started, at the mercy of the hated Oligarchy. The locked-out workers were then brought back into the factories (reportedly by gangster tactics) where they were encouraged to get production going again. On orders from Perón, one of the tactics used to make them return to the factories and keep them at work even against their will – since many were justifiably frightened to be seen defying the factory owners – was the deliberate flooding of their homes by the Fire Department. This drove whole families, who might otherwise have resisted, back to work. The Employers' Strike was smashed.

While frightened citizens continued to queue or fight for places on the steamers to Montevideo and while Peronist thugs were breaking up opposition meetings with clubs, axe handles and knuckledusters, Evita was not lying low. Indeed, aware that about one in every five Argentinians was illiterate and therefore totally dependent upon the radio for news, she had been working relentlessly in that area. Still employed by Radio Belgrano, which she now controlled almost totally, she was also Perón's official publicity officer as well as his wife, and did not hesitate to use the stream of broadcasting 'regulations' that had been pouring out of President Farrell's Perón-dominated offices to deny radio access to opposing parties whenever possible. She also spoke a lot herself, taught Perón the tricks of broadcasting, and in general ensured that Peronism dominated the airwaves.

Finally, on election day, no strong-arm tactics were required to collect Perón's votes. The previous barrage of demagogy and violent persuasion had managed to eliminate all opposition. On 24 February 1946, the male citizens of Argentina, by an honest vote, elected Juan Domingo Perón as their President.

That night, the celebrations in Buenos Aires were spectacular. Food and wine were lavished upon the Peronist supporters, oxen were barbecued in the streets and parks, and dancing and singing continued until dawn.

The day Perón became their legal President, more than a million Argentines roared with unquenchable enthusiasm. Packed in behind the rows of steel-helmeted, bayonet-bearing soldiers who lined the Avenida de Mayo from the Chamber of Deputies to the Casa Rosada, the ecstatic *descamisados* waved and cheered and threw flowers. At the stroke of midday, resplendent in the blue-gold-encrusted dress uniform of a brigadier-general, Perón strode into the great hall of Congress, surrounded by beribboned generals and starched diplomats. Smiling from her special box was the alabaster beauty, Señora Perón, beloved as 'Evita'. Sitting close to her, his many medals glittering, was Constatin V. Sheveley, commercial representative of the Soviet Union, who had just announced the resumption of relations between Russia and Argentina. Later would come the drive to the Casa Rosada, between the blue-and-white-striped

Argentine flags and, in the blue gloom of the Casa Rosada's white salon, surrounded by grenadiers in uniforms of the Independence period (blue tunics, red-striped trousers, red pompom-topped shakos), the handing of the mace from the tearful ex-President Edelmiro Farrell to the solemn-faced, inwardly jovial President Perón.

Evita was now the First Lady of Argentina.

Chapter Ten

Shortly after meeting Juan Perón, Evita made her final two films: *La Cabalgata del Circo* (*The Cavalcade of the Circus*) and *La Prodiga* (*The Spendthrift*). The latter had a title so prophetic as to be miraculous, but instead of being released it was given to President Perón as a 'personal gift' from the producers. The former, a critical and box-office disaster, was one of many movies starring Eva Duarte that the more dignified Evita would have destroyed. From this point on, she would make no more movies, though in truth she would never stop acting.

In fact, Evita had made a great number of movies, most of them bad, a series of historical romances filled with drama and great achievements of the kind she had imagined in her childhood. On the radio and in cinema she had played the great women of history and other, fictional, women of singular achievement. Now, as the line between theatricality and real life became blurred in her mind, she created a composite of all her favourite characters and gradually turned this magical creature into the one who would soon become widely known as *Santa* (Saint) Evita.

'She created a character,' said Señor Julio Alcaraz, her regular hairdresser. 'In her public life she created a character for herself, and she lived this character totally.'

Undoubtedly this was true. From the moment Eva Duarte took up with Colonel Perón, the remaining shreds of her more human side were stripped away. Evita now loved Perón as the child Eva had loved her daydreams, seeing neither reality nor truth: only the possibility of glory in the eyes of her lover. If Perón had once been flesh and blood, he had since gone beyond that: he was the miracle of a dream made manifest, his destiny mapped out. Evita shared that destiny. The country's heart beat in her breast. She and Perón and Argentina – the Holy Trinity – were one and the same. For this reason her love for Perón, which was a passion like no other, had changed into something more noble than the body's base hunger.

I was not just the wife of the President of the Republic; I was also the wife of the Leader of the Argentinian people . . . I feel as though I am the real mother of my nation . . . Perhaps I don't suffer with it? Perhaps I don't enjoy its happiness? Perhaps its griefs do not grieve me? Perhaps my blood doesn't race when it is insulted or criticised? My loves are its loves. For this reason I love Perón in a different way to that in which I used to. Before I loved him for himself. Now I love him because his people love him!

What greater love than this? What country could ask for more? If Evita was to be childless, if her rumoured distaste for sex was fact, was it not also true that, when she made love to Perón, she could enjoy it only because she felt that through him she was making love to the nation? Some said she was the nation's whore. Others claimed she was the nation's mother. So through Perón she made love to the nation and gave birth to the future. If sexless, she had emotion. Or, like an actress, she *conveyed* emotion. Once Eva, now Evita, that more intimate 'little Eva', she would encourage her people to view her as both mother and mistress.

When I chose to be 'Evita' I knew I was choosing the path of my people. Now, after making that choice, it is easy for me to show that this was the case. Only the people call me 'Evita'. Only the *descamisados* learnt to call me that. Government ministers, political leaders, ambassadors, businessmen, professionals and intellectuals and all the others who visit me usually call me 'Madam'; and when in public some of them say, 'Your most excellent and worthy ladyship', or sometimes, 'Lady President'. They only see me as Eva Perón. On the other hand, the poor only want to know me as 'Evita'. That's how I introduced myself to them when I went to meet the poor of my country; saying that I would prefer to be 'Evita', rather than the President's wife, if this 'Evita' could help relieve any grief or dry any tears.

Evita's conviction that she represented the soul of her country began during her days as Perón's mistress. Now, as the First Lady of Argentina, her belief in the power of the working masses confirmed, she set out to become the most powerful woman in Latin America and, eventually, the world.

Afire with the revealed love of her loyal *descamisados*, moved by the conviction that she represented the New (Peronist) Argentina, she wasted no time in turning her flamboyant dreams into reality.

Soon after taking over the Presidency, Juan Perón

gave his wife a desk and a few 'small chores' to do at the Secretariat of Labour, his old post. Within weeks, the Secretary of Labour was simply running Evita's errands while Evita got on with running the whole show. Before a month had passed, seasoned politicians who had thought of Evita as no more than an ambitious 'little whore' were learning, frequently to their cost, that she was tough, shrewd and ruthless.

Adapting the same dawn-to-dusk working routine as her husband, she interviewed hundreds of people weekly and travelled all over Argentina, making speeches at countless union rallies. In no time at all, she had taken over the management of the rowdy but loving *descamisados* from Perón, seducing them into submission with her charm and generosity, thinking rarely of the consequences of what she was giving away, only concerned with the immediate, invariably warm, response.

The response was always the same, though it grew ever warmer. Soon the workers thronging in May Square, instead of chanting 'Perón! Perón!', were chanting 'Evita! Evita!' until the latter took precedence over the former. And, under her alluring command, the once-powerful General Confederation of Labour became a docile Peronist instrument, reduced to carrying out orders and staging mass demonstrations in the Square.

'She's worth more to me than five ministers,' Perón announced.

Under Evita's direction, Perón had made political capital during his Presidential campaign out of designating women's suffrage a basic plank in the Perón platform. Now Evita, a woman with no female friends, was using women's suffrage to strengthen her position with the underprivileged. Adding a votes-for-women campaign to her long list of public activities, she also broadcast in its favour every Wednesday night from Radio Belgrano. Not content with this, she 'bought' control of the newspaper, *Democracia*, and entered the publishing field, kicking off with a new daily column: 'The Argentine Woman Wants to Vote'. By now she had also gained indirect control of the principal Argentine newsreel companies and was ensuring that she appeared at least two or three times in every newsreel, usually against background scenes of other women and children, and invariably proclaiming the right of women to vote.

This gambit was no accident. Like the good public performer she was, Evita knew that much of her appeal lay in her good looks and that her major support, which came from the macho workers, had incidentally caused resentment amongst their women. By liberating women, and by her forthcoming acts of charity, she was not only widening the broad base of her support, but also strengthening her image as a saint. Because of this, she became a heroine to her formerly oppressed countrywomen.

'Evita represents the authentic symbol of the Argentinian woman,' said Ebe Bedrune, a popular young bandleader, 'because, above all else, she has not lost her feeling for humanity.' And regarding Evita's fight for women's rights: 'She is the first girl, if I may call her that, who has elevated our thoughts and taught us our mission as citizens.'

Ostensibly a women's liberationist (before the term became fashionable in the West), Evita was actually laying the groundwork for a pro-Perón (thus pro-Evita) Women's Party. Yet to say this might well be an injustice, since, if Evita was many things (cold, cal-culating, shrewish, vindictive), she was also genuinely involved in the plight of her countrywomen. Her own past – with its hardships and humiliations, its revela-tions of how an Argentine woman would always be a second-class citizen, mere chattel to men, forced to beg and surrender her honour for what she needed – had imbued her with this singular passion.

Even though her economic ignorance, distorted view of social justice and vengeful nature would even-tually lead the country to near ruination, her passion for women's rights was sincere. Like many a woman who has been used by many men, Evita both despised and was totally dependent upon the male sex. Though her steely resolve and unwavering ambition in a man's world had divorced her from close friendships with other women, she continued to despise men for how they had used her and, aware that other women had suffered similarly, she sympathised with women in general. Indeed, one of her few legitimate triumphs was won in September 1947 when her bill giving women in Argentina the right to vote was approved.

However, by late 1946 Evita was still rushing breathlessly through her new career as First Lady of Argentina. In her office on the fourth floor of the Central Post Office Building she was receiving trade union delegations before her bourgeois neighbours (who despised her) had risen from their beds in the swank houses along the Avenida Alvear. Cabinet ministers eager to hear and kowtow to her views, teachers and nurses quick to note a militant feminist, ragged mothers from poor villages, hungry gauchos from the pampas, and trade union leaders seeking pay rises for their workers poured daily into her jammed waiting rooms. When not dealing with these humble souls, Evita would be sitting in on conferences to debate her husband's latest labour policy or the government's anti-inflation campaign, much to the annoyance of the other cabinet ministers – an annoyance they dared not show.

Abused and used in childhood and adolescence, Evita had come to understand the mechanics of power and the value of having trustworthy friends placed in useful positions. It did not pass unnoticed that her playboy brother, Juan Duarte, had quickly been elected as her private secretary. Nor that Evita was surreptitiously surrounding the President with more and more of her own men, most of them servile mediocrities who would leap to obey her. Thus well guarded from the rear, she could turn her pretty face towards the masses awaiting her ministrations. And the public and private faces of Evita were two different masks.

'It wasn't difficult to publicise Eva Perón,' said Raul Apold, the Press and Propaganda Secretary, 'given that she gave so much. During the Presidential campaign she was really Perón's backbone. For the people she was part of their flesh and blood. Especially in the interior, where they had real admiration for this young girl with her smile and her strong, piercing eyes. Eva wasn't worried if she made enemies herself, but she couldn't forgive those who were enemies of her husband.'

The public Evita was the soul of saintliness and generosity, but the private Evita was a different person altogether. She enjoyed taking revenge for all the real or imagined wrongs done to her and now, with her authority and power, she set out to do so.

Señor Yankelevich of Radio Belgrano had already suffered at Evita's tender hands and now two of the country's most popular actresses, Dolores del Rio and Amanda Ledesman, found themselves in a similar position. Ledesman, who had been the star of a radio show in which Evita appeared during her early years in Buenos Aires, suddenly found radio work unobtainable. As for Dolores del Rio, she was already successful in the Hollywood despised by Evita because it has so consistently rejected her. So, for some real or imagined slight, dating back to when she was working in a picture in which Dolores del Rio was starring, Evita had the actress barred from all Argentine studios. Eventually, North American producers came to realise that US movies featuring Dolores del Rio were no longer being bought by Argentine cinemas.

Amongst others forced out of Argentina by Evita were: Huge del Carrill, who had pinned a facetious note on Evita's first mink coat in a Buenos Aires nightclub; Nina Marshall, the Argentine's leading radio and film star, who had made the mistake of imitating Evita at parties; and Pedro Cuartucci, who had refused to sing a serenade on the balcony of the Casa Rosada on the day of Perón's liberation from prison. Likewise, while Evita would greet the poor and the humble with a radiant smile and a willing chequebook, she would coldly abuse and then dismiss any non-union worker or middle-class professional in her presence.

This private Evita – the one who needed revenge for all real or imagined slights and who had to destroy all those opposed to Perón/Evita – was now about to embark on the most flamboyant escapade of her political career: the infamous Rainbow Tour.

*

If Evita had been accepted by the *descamisados* as their saviour and Lady of Hope, she was still despised by the wealthy of Buenos Aires (the Oligarchy) who could not forgive her for her common background and her early years as an actress, regarding her as a vulgar, ambitious tramp. In a sense, while Evita had won the love of the *descamisados*, she had still not proved herself as a woman fit to be the President's wife. It was perhaps because of this that Evita began to dress more lavishly in public, to adorn herself with all the regalia of a Great Lady, dressed primarily by Christian Dior, wrapped in other glittering gowns by Fath and Rochas and Balmain, in expensive furs and extraordinary jewellery. No longer a Lana Turner lookalike in period costume, she was now more in the line of an Argentinian Grace Kelly, she of *The Swan*, a blonde-haired, crystalline beauty of the most asexual kind. In doing this, she was seeking to impersonate and, perhaps, equal the very people she most despised: the wealthy, snobbish women of the Oligarchy. So far it hadn't worked.

However, Evita also had another reason for the Rainbow Tour. Much of her growing popularity at this time was due to her cleverly staged public acts of charity towards the poor. Though other, more reputable, charity organisations had been doing their work quietly for years, Evita was now putting them in the shade by ensuring that her own good deeds were widely publicised. (Her personal photographer was never absent when she dished out the money.) More vitally, she had already started wresting control from many of the other charities and was using her authority to do them serious damage. The most important of these charities was the Sociedad de Beneficencia

(Society of Philanthropy), which was run by the female social elite of Buenos Aires. The perennial president of the organisation was the wealthy Señora Maria Unzue de Alvear; but the post of honorary secretary was traditionally reserved for the wife of Argentina's President, who was, at this particular time, Evita. Evita wanted the post, but the women of the society refused to offer her the position, making it clear that they still despised her as a commoner.

It was Evita's intention to force the snobbish upper crust of Argentine society to receive her socially, primarily by electing her as honorary president of the Sociedad de Beneficencia, and she felt that she could do this by courting the crowned heads of Europe and returning to Argentina as an honoured lady. The Rainbow Tour was therefore, at bottom, a self-serving public-relations campaign.

'I send you my rainbow,' President Perón cabled to the Spanish government.

Evita left on her Rainbow Tour in June 1947, reportedly with five dozen lavish costumes, enough jewellery to sink a battleship, and a considerable amount of Argentinian pesos *in cash*. Stopping first in Spain, she passed on the regards of one dictator to another by saying to General Franco: 'I did not come here to establish an axis, but only as a rainbow between our two countries.' General Franco, a wily old fox, awarded the mink-coated beauty the Cross of Isabel La Catolica and sent her out to greet the worshipful Spaniards. The Spaniards, ever enamoured with women who wore ostrich plumes and mink, gave her a rapturous reception while she dispensed gifts of hard cash to the tune of over £1,000 per day.

It was all downhill after that.

From Spain she went to Italy where, from the balcony of a forty-room mansion that had cost Perón's Embassy in Rome £100,000 to prepare, she was shocked by the roars of, 'Down with Perón! Down with Argentina! Down with Fascism!' Undeterred, she went on to an audience with Pope Pius XII, from whom she hoped to receive the highest papal decoration, the supreme Order of Christ. Instead, after an audience of thirty minutes, she was awarded the Grand Cross of the Order of Pius IX, a magnificent, diamond-studded, eight-pointed star that was, nonetheless, only second in the papal hierarchy. As if this were not enough, when she then visited Northern Italy, the communists bawled obscenities, most notably by calling her a whore. Shocked again, Evita turned to her official escort, a former senior naval officer who slyly ground salt into her wounds by murmuring, 'Think nothing of it, my dear. I haven't been to sea for fifteen years and they still call me an admiral.' Finally, after Evita had suffered a merciless grilling by the press, some American GIs showed their own kind of respect with wolf whistles. Simultaneously outraged and humiliated, Evita left Italy and travelled on to France.

In Paris, after being received by President Vincent Auriol and other leading dignitaries, she witnessed the signing of a Franco-Argentinian commercial treaty, extending a loan of £150,750,000 to France. However, if the glamour-smitten Spaniards had given her a rapturous reception, the more sophisticated French were less impressed. After Evita had obliged the photographers (she was always more keen on photographers than on journalists, as is the case with most actresses) by showing off the furs, gowns, hats and shoes that she had acquired in an orgy of shopping, one member of the French press was moved to write: 'Madam Perón would be more palatable to the French workers and peasants if she were dressed as a piece of Argentinian frozen beef.' Following this, she had her windscreen smashed and the car windows cracked by an expertly thrown brick and was then grossly insulted in a Paris nightclub. Subsequently, though compelled to remain for some time in Paris, *La Bella Blonde d'Argentina* lost her enthusiasm and, suddenly tired and pale, her smile infinitely more painful, started cancelling appointments and waited listlessly for a call from the Queen of England.

Evita was expecting to be invited to stay in Buckingham Palace as a house guest – the one thing that would finally force the ladies of the Avenida Alvear to accept her and make her honorary president of the Sociedad de Beneficencia – but, alas, such was not to be the case. After a lot of hedging by the guardians of the Palace, she was finally invited merely to take tea with the Queen. Furious, she resolved to return home.

Something else might have disturbed her during her stay in Paris. Throughout the period she was there, her activities were being watched by Perón's Secret Service and reported back to Argentine's Government House in Buenos Aires. It is possible that Evita found out about this, since her brother, Juan Duarte, also close to Perón, was travelling with her. What Evita *did* know is that Perón had made his first world broadcast in her absence and that he had, subsequently, taken to the air in a big way. In fact, Perón was to make over one hundred broadcasts during 1947 and many of them were made, often to be broadcast much later, during Evita's seemingly convenient absence. Evita, therefore, with her passion for personally controlling the Argentinian airwaves, might have felt resentment and possibly even fear at learning what her husband had been up to behind her back. Certainly, later, there would be many ominous rumours of private rifts between her and her husband.

No official explanation was offered in Argentina for the fact that Evita and her brother made a brief trip to Switzerland. Though it was hardly mentioned by the press, a number of Argentinian officials would later suspect that the trip had been made for the purpose of setting up Evita's notorious Swiss bank account.

Whatever the purpose of her visit, Evita soon returned from Switzerland and then left Paris quietly, without the cheers and boos of Madrid and Rome respectively, slipping away as if she had never been. After dallying briefly on the Riveria (where, for the first time, she deliberately avoided the press photographers), she returned to Argentina by way of Brazil. In Rio de Janeiro, where she attended the Inter-American Joint Defence Conference, the streets were covered with thousands of huge posters of her, most of which the Brazilian police hastily tore down. Finally, smiling brightly and denying her true lack of spirit, she returned to a triumphant welcome in Buenos Aires, where Perón gave a passionate public speech and Evita, also in public, wept for joy.

The Rainbow Tour made Evita's fame (or infamy) known worldwide, but it still did not gain her the honorary presidency of the Sociedad de Beneficencia. It was out of this dogmatic refusal, this all too public sign of the Oligarchy's contempt for the 'little whore', that Evita's most obsessive lust for vengeance and total power was born.

Less than a year later, she had killed off the historical Sociedad de Beneficencia, replaced it with 'the biggest racket the world has known in our time', and finally, with a malice that knew no bounds, refused permission for the remains of the recently deceased President of the society, Señora Maria Unzue de Alvear, to be buried next to those of her husband in the family tomb of a church that had been founded and built by Señora de Alvear out of her own purse.

Evita, having proved that she could not be scorned, turned her back on the ruin she had wreaked and went on to bigger things.

Chapter Eleven

The Peróns' method of consolidating their power was simply to take care of everyone who supported them, irrespective of the future cost. Perón spent lavishly on the army and allowed, or didn't dare stop, Evita's own extravagant spending. The basic *modus operandi* was to offer a public spectacle of generosity, keep everyone happy, strengthen their popularity with the workers, and let the future take care of itself. Because of this, by early 1948 Perón had not only spent the whole of Argentina's war profits, but had also, with his grandiose expansionist schemes, run the country £500 million into debt.

Evita's personal contribution to this immediately beneficial and ultimately disastrous form of government was to shower pesos like pennies from heaven on the eternally grateful *descamisados*. When the Railway Union asked for a 40 per cent rise, Evita generously gave them 50 per cent. When the telephone operators planned to get half of 70 per cent, Evita nobly gave them the lot. Already, in her offices in the Ministry of Labour and Welfare, she was handing out money indiscriminately – or at least as she herself saw fit. Not only was she signing cheques by the dozen, but the sight of a pleading face before her would encourage her to pull a wad of pesos from her desk drawer and shove them into the hand of the astonished recipient. Evita was also starting to ignore the need for records of such transactions. Where the money came from might be something that interested her; what clearly did not concern her was where it might come from in the future.

Determined to fix the 'old hags' of the Oligarchy for good, Evita, on 23 June 1947, brought the portentously entitled Maria Eva Duarte de Perón Social Aid Foundation into being. Aware of the power that such a charity could bring her, she first removed every competitor in private welfare and crushed their hated bones beneath the weight of her own ambitions. The Maria Eva Duarte de Perón Social Aid Foundation reportedly started with a mere £750 of Evita's own money, began its life in the General Post Office building, moved on to the larger Secretariat of Labour and Welfare, and then, about eighteen months later, was moved into an extraordinary Grecian-styled building, seven storeys high, fronted by marble columns topped by a number of statues. The whole building filled an entire city block.

The initial £750 was dramatically increased by the expropriation of huge sums of money from the various trade unions, the reluctant businessmen, and finally from the workers as well. Few of these contributors were volunteers.

On Labour Day, 1 May 1951, by order of the General Confederation of Labour (virtually controlled by Evita), every worker in the country was required to hand over a full day's earnings to the Foundation. Shortly after, the civil servants were 'encouraged' to hand over ten per cent of their combined annual salaries to the Foundation and did so, with a fat cheque, at a public demonstration in the Colon Theatre, Buenos Aires. More money was extracted from the major employers by 'persuading' them to pay by 'lunar' months and donating the cheque for the thirteenth month of the year to the Foundation.

In 1951 it would not have been considered safe to even *think* of criticising the Foundation; and many famous and anonymous citizens of Argentina were hounded into exile for having made the mistake of doing just that.

(Richard Balbin, leader of the Radical Party, said in a speech to the House of Deputies: 'The public charities of the President's wife seem to rebound to her private good.' He was subsequently sentenced, after eight months' wait in jail, to five years' imprisonment for 'disrespect towards the President and other un-Argentine activities'.)

Other methods of extortion (called 'voluntary donations') abounded. For instance, employees of the Banco Central *not* wishing to donate one day's pay to the Foundation were to notify the Board of Management *in writing*. Likewise, when the young winner of a radio contest stated that he was not going to hand over his winnings to the Foundation, Evita's Publicity Office put out the news that the entire audience at the contest had broken into tears upon hearing the young man's selfish refusal. It was not reported just how this particular offender was punished for his disrespect and lack of public feeling, but certainly all future winnings were turned over to the Foundation and the winners received only a personal note of thanks from the First Lady.

By mid-1951, government lotteries and gambling casinos had also come under the hammer and were reported to have 'contributed' 36,458,296 pesos during the first six months of the year; casinos not contributing would soon have their licences revoked for 'unlawful practices'. Likewise, when a large manufacturer of chocolates refused to contribute, he was visited by three municipal sanitary inspectors who found his factory to be insanitary and closed it down for all time. Thereafter, industrialists in the Argentine more readily handed over the cash.

Eschewing the more blatant forms of suppression, such as concentration camps, Evita and Perón nevertheless crushed resistance to their government with lengthy jail sentences, by ruining opponents economically or by harassing them until they fled across the river to Uruguay. Evita had already displayed her penchant for 'legal' suppression by financially ruining all charities except her own, by gaining control of all the newsreel companies, and by wresting direct control of the newspapers *Democracia*, *Laborista* and *Noticias Graficas*. (By this time, expanding her business interests, she also owned a medical, surgical, mathematical and scientific instrument company and was setting up an agricultural product company under her own name.) Criticism of Perón's government, or of Evita's scandalous Foundation, was therefore rendered furtive and highly dangerous. While Perón was packing the courts and universities with his stooges, encouraging Congress to vote him absolute power over his seventeen million people, including the right to jail them for 'disrespect' (an abstraction beyond all possibility of defence), Evita was ensuring silence by the 'legal' suppression of any organisation antagonistic to her.

As we have seen, foremost among the victims were various leading Argentine newspapers and *La Razon*, the prominent Buenos Aires daily that had long been openly hostile to the Peróns, became the next, and the biggest, to fall. Determined to ruin *La Razon*, a team of Evita's municipal inspectors constantly harassed the paper's offices, first accusing the accountants of keeping inaccurate accounts (untrue), then inspecting the washrooms, lifts and fire extinguishers (all in order), then fining the proprietors hundreds of thousands of pesos for minor infractions and, finally, claiming a major sanitary violation because an office fan was too small. *La Razon* paid up, dropped its editorial page, and for the first time in its illustrious history expressed no opinions of any kind about anything. Later, to the horror of many Argentinians, *La Razon* was closed down entirely.

Nor did it end there. The *Argentine Libre* was suddenly told by its printer in Buenos Aires that he could no longer handle the paper. The owner promptly found another small printing shop in La Plata, thirty-five miles from the capital; but, after the La Plata shop had brought out one issue, it was closed by municipal authorities because it 'lacked proper washroom facilities'. Another leading opposition paper, the Socialist Party's *La Vanguardia*, was closed because the sound of its printing presses at night violated a municipal anti-noise measure; the loading of papers into delivery trucks tied up traffic on the block; and the press room lacked first-aid equipment.

Finally, since Perón's government controlled the flow of newsprint, it could and did divert it from unfriendly to friendly papers. And since, due to the nationalisation of the banks in March 1946, all bank loans had to be cleared through the Banco Central of Argentina, any newspaper antagonistic to Evita/ Perón would have found it impossible to obtain even a routine loan. The Post Office, also, had often refused to distribute newspapers expressing anti-Peronist views.

The creation of an Undersecretariat of Press and Radio sealed up the remaining gaps in this massive suppression. The Undersecretariat's job was to take a personal interest in 'the type and tone' of political news, which meant in effect that free access to primary news sources was increasingly denied to news reporters. More and more, they were forced to rely on handouts from the Undersecretariat; and official press conferences would consist of the distribution of mimeographed communiqués presenting the government point of view. Due to the Undersecretariat, further loss of freedom of expression was ensured by the limiting of the licence system for radio stations. Since all stations had to operate under temporary licences granted by the government, it was easy to make them understand that the broadcasting of anti-Peronist news or opinions would lead to a revocation of their licences. It was also made clear that no one could speak against the President, his wife or the government as a whole, and that commentators could only say what they were *for*. On the other hand, three times a day, without paying for the air time, the government broadcast its own news programme over every station in Argentina.

Though this massive repression was going on daily, it was scarcely noticed by the majority of working Argentinians. Formerly either ignored entirely or ruthlessly exploited by the Oligarchy and successive governments, the workers now had, in Perón and in his saintly wife, Evita, staunch defenders of their livelihood and future. Suddenly, after years of being treated like slave labour, they saw their wages doubled and even trebled, they were receiving bonuses and paid holidays, and summer camps and rest homes were being built for them.

However, if the workers were happy, the regime's opponents were more concerned, pointing out the high cost of these so-called gains. In many cases the rise in the cost of living had paralleled, and sometimes exceeded, the wage increases. It was also noted that the benefits won by the unions had been gained at the cost of their independence. In particular, the General Confederation of Labour, once the most powerful union in the country, had been reduced to a mere chattel of the government and was now conducting most of its business (which was Perón's business) in a room in the Casa Rosada. There, three military men on Perón's staff, with the help of a mimeograph machine and the Confederation's stationery, issued Labour edicts and Labour news that had been written by Evita's Publicity Office. A further source of irritation was that those unions that played the government's game had little difficulty in getting what they wanted, whereas the unions that tried to maintain a measure of independence found themselves unable to function freely.

One of Perón's many methods of breaking independent unions was the use of the so-called Federal Intervenor, whose job was to manage the affairs of the union on behalf of the government. One such union, the fifty-year-old Union of Office Workers of Cordoba Province, was 'intervened' in January 1948, after which it had its charter annulled and its right to represent the workers cancelled. Likewise, while a group of pro-Perón industrialists were enjoying special 'under-the-table' privileges, the ordinary businessmen, or those antagonistic to Peronism, were finding themselves controlled at every turn and having to operate under a law, designed to forbid 'speculation', that was so vague as to render day-to-day dealings almost impossible. So, too, did the universities find themselves short of many able professors, who had either been forced to resign or prematurely 'retired'.

Finally, to ensure that the courts could not redress any of these Peronist wrongs, Perón had Congress throw out three of the more difficult judges and filled their seats with his friends. (One of these was Justo Rodriguez, the husband of Evita's sister, Blanca.) When doing so, he always made a point of firing judges who had jurisdiction over civil rights. Given this knowledge, as well as the fact that those who remained would not want the same medicine, it was a foregone conclusion that the courts would support all future attempts to suppress newspapers, radio stations and recalcitrant trade unions – and this is precisely what they did.

To all intents and purposes, Argentina was now totally controlled by Juan Perón and Evita.

Chapter Twelve

With all means of criticising them throttled, Juan Perón and Evita could now smother the whole country in marshmallow. Perón's official plans to beat inflation and Evita's more personal plans for the Eva Perón Foundation were sold with the aid of an extensive, relentless publicity campaign. Indeed, the public love affair between the President and his wife was as carefully orchestrated as one of the overheated Argentinian movies that Evita, when plain Eva Duarte, had formerly starred in. The story, not uncommon in those kinds of movie, went something like this . . .

Little Eva is born of poor parents in the pampas – a true *descamisado* – and grows up to be a beautiful, blonde teenager who attracts the beastly attentions of many men. After suffering the common woes of the 'shirtless ones', she leaves the farm and travels to the Big City where, after many hardships and humiliations, sexual and otherwise, she turns herself, Cinderella fashion, into a sophisticated young woman. She becomes a movie star, finds fame and fortune, but also learns that it is Lonely at the Top. Luckily, the dashing, macho army officer, Juan Perón, now enters the picture and, as befits this traditional movie, it is Love at First Sight.

('I saw him appear,' says Evita in her fanciful memoirs. 'He stood out from all the others. They would cry "Fire!" and order the advance; he cried "Fire!"

and advanced himself, determinedly and relentlessly in one direction, without faltering at any obstacle. In that moment I felt his war cry and his path were my own.')

Also born in the pampas but now high up in the army, little Eva's handsome lover, Colonel Juan Perón, is a macho man, a war hero and a playboy irresistible to women. Nevertheless, deep down, he is dissatisfied with his hedonistic life and is in search of his Destiny. He meets little Eva, now a glamorous, famous lady, and his love for her changes him overnight and makes him a better man. She reminds him that both of them come from the pampas and that fame and fortune cannot replace the love they once received from their own kind, namely the shirtless ones. Perón is transformed! Now dedicated to his country, but seeing injustice on all sides, he becomes a Friend to the People, is jailed by the ruling junta, and sends his devotion to the shirtless ones through his beloved Eva, writing faithfully from the darkness of his prison cell.

('I searched eagerly through his letters for words of love,' says Evita in her memoirs. 'Instead, he spoke of hardly anything except his "workers", who, when they were loose on the streets, he had begun to call *descamisados*. Entrusting me with his "workers" were his words of love, his most deeply felt words of love. As long as I live, I shall never forget that.')

Little Eva, who loves Perón, who in his turn loves the people through little Eva, arouses the *descamisados* to demonstrate for his release from prison. The Friend to the People is duly released. He then overthrows the corrupt ruling government, takes over the country, pours his contempt on the Oligarchy, and brings Justice and Prosperity to the *descamisados* . . . And beside him, radiantly beautiful, but also humble, even saintlike, is little Eva, now the glamorous Evita, whose love is eternal.

('I am only a humble woman,' says Evita in her memoirs, 'a swallow amongst a vast flock of swallows. He was, and still is, the giant eagle flying safely high among the clouds, close to God. If it were not for the way he swooped down to my level and taught me to fly differently, I would never have known what an eagle is, nor would I have been able to contemplate the magnificent extent of my people. Because of this, neither my life nor my heart belong to me. Nothing I am or possess is mine. All I am, all I own, all I think and all I feel belongs to Perón.')

The violins soar. The sun glints in Evita's blonde hair. She stands beside the dashing President, her husband, Juan Perón, on the balcony of the Casa Rosada, as the cheers of their beloved *descamisados* lift them up in a great spiritual wave to the right hand of God. Love and loyalty conquer all . . .

The public, the great mass of *descamisados*, could not resist it. They were being swamped by the greatest soap opera of their times and it had them enthralled.

Central to the growth of this nauseating spectacle was the Eva Perón Publicity Office. Organised by this office were the huge posters of Evita and Perón that soon covered every wall in Buenos Aires. Written by that same office were the countless propaganda speeches that were delivered histrionically week after week by Perón or Evita. Still enamoured of the style of his old hero, Mussolini, Perón would thunder and roar, his coat off and his sleeves rolled up, one hand placed over his heart or else balled in a fist that slammed up and down as he raved. And beside him, little Eva, the *campañera Evita*, her large brown eyes flashing, blonde hair shining, body trembling; first humbly lowering her head, her voice a tremulous whisper, then suddenly straightening up, punching the air with her fists, all fire and fury, sometimes weeping with emotion, flaunting diamonds and sables and Christian Dior gowns as she told the ragged workers: 'I was once just as you are now! I am taking these jewels from the Oligarchy only for you! *All* of you! One day you will inherit this whole treasure! You will *all* have clothes like these!' And the *descamisados*, the shirtless ones, now drunk with emotion, believing her every word, would stumble away from May Square and look up at the countless posters saying 'Perón Fulfils His Promises' or 'Juan and Eva – a Blessed Couple' or 'Evita We Love You' or 'Evita is Love' and they would sob with pride and joy.

Who could resist it? What mere mortal could withstand it? The Argentinians are in love with the very idea of love, and this great love between their President and his wife, their adored Evita, was all-embracing and perfect.

If Evita had once been a second-rate actress, she had now, by sheer tenacity and cunning, won her Academy Award.

'It struck me as a kind of popular Vaudeville,' said Sir John Balfour, then the British Ambassador in Argentina, 'with Perón as the stage manager and Eva as the lead actress. Perón . . . put her on the stage.'

The main stage for Evita's histrionics was undoubtedly the Maria Eva Duarte de Perón Social Aid

Foundation. Now the most influential woman in the hemisphere – hailed in Argentina as being in a class with Eleanor Roosevelt, Madame Chiang Kai-shek, and the consort of the Grand Mufti of Jerusalem; awarded, on top of her previous accolades, with the Dominican Republic's Grand Cross of the Order of Juan Pablo Duarte (no relation) and Bolivia's Order of the Condor of the Andes; hailed by her own citizens as *la Dama de la Esperanza* (the Lady of Hope) – Evita had become obsessed with her own image as a saint and was tireless in attending to her flock.

'She worked fourteen or fifteen hours a day,' said Atilio Renzi, her private secretary. 'It was quite common to finish at three or four in the morning and be back at work at seven thirty.'

Up and dressed by six o'clock in the morning, Evita would drive in her Rolls-Royce three times a week to her rooms in the Secretariat of Labour and Welfare. There she would hold a bizarre court to listen to the problems of the poor, the sick, the lame and the old. On each of these occasions the corridors leading to the 'Charity Court' would be jammed tight with humble and conniving supplicants. A corps of secretaries, male and female, always flanked Evita's desk, the most prominent feature of which was a large alms box. Apart from an oil painting by one Juan Carlos Alonso, the only other pictures on the walls were of the Peróns – and, perhaps deliberately, of Christ.

The supplicants would approach the Christlike Evita at her desk and pour out their troubles. If the problem was money, one of Evita's secretaries would reach into the alms box and hand over at least a one-hundred-peso note. If, on the other hand, the problem was something else, that would be dealt with as well.

If a man needed a job, a job was found for him. (The chosen employer would not dare to refuse him work.) If a woman's husband had deserted her, Evita's strong men would seek him out. (The erring husband would rarely refuse to return home.) If someone owed rent, the required sum would be provided and the 'victimising' landlord reprimanded (even if in the right). Evita also had on her staff some strong-arm 'charity men' whose job was to locate drunken husbands and more or less beat some sense into them. Evita personally ordered clothing, bedding and furniture for those who needed it; and she personally wrote prescriptions for drugs. In short, whatever the case, Evita *worked*.

The sublime inanity of the Social Aid Foundation was to be found in the fact that it was not obliged to keep records of its spending. It was also ludicrous in that the enormous annual contributions (received through legalised forms of extortion) were not being invested in more far-ranging or long-term projects but were being dispensed with random generosity to whoever managed to get an audience with Evita. In actuality, therefore, the Social Aid Foundation was, on the one hand, Evita's greatest act of vengeance against the now obsolete Sociedad de Beneficencia's 'haughty dowagers' and, on the other, a massively organised propaganda platform from which the beloved *Primera Dama* could launch herself forth into sainthood.

The Señora's desk was set up under floodlights [John Dos Passos recorded] behind a big bronze oversize bust of some hero of Argentine independence ... When she finally arrived the floodlights were turned on and there was a great rush of cameramen in the narrow room. Distinguished visitors were posed in an admiring group behind the Señora's handsome blonde head as she leaned over the desk to listen to the troubles of the poor women with their tear-stained children . . . When a delegation of businessmen appeared with a cheque in five figures for the Señora's Foundation all other business was suspended while the cameramen posed the group. The cheque had to appear in the photograph. The Señora's white hand was held out to receive it. The leader of the delegation was presenting it with a deferential bow.

Indeed, behind the façade of charity, when the women and their weeping children had departed, '*Santa*' Evita would show herself as someone quite different. Dos Passos also recorded that 'with her secretaries and the government officials her manner was domineering, the manner of a rich hostess ordering the help about, but with the delegates it was level and sisterly.' So she hid behind two masks. One was cruel and one was kind. But the kindness was reserved solely for formal public appearances, while in private the political animal took precedence. In the words of the journalist James Cameron: 'When I first met her in the plushy wonders of the world's most opulent Ministry of Employment, it was like looking into the eyes of Rita Hayworth and finding Aneurin Bevan looking out of them.' The radiance of those eyes, which gazed in a kindly manner from the city's hoardings, did not reflect the real, much harder Evita.

[Perón] was down to earth, cynical, realistic [said

Sir John Balfour] and I can't say that when we were talking together *her* sentiments were exactly gentle and soft. At one moment she said to me – she was making up, incidentally, just before rising to her feet to make her after-luncheon speech – and she said to me, 'You know I love a fight. If there weren't a fight I'd have to invent one. And if it hadn't been for Perón' – who had been sitting beside her, and she gave him a nudge as she said this – 'I would have been the revolutionary out on the barricades, stringing all the Oligarchs up by the neck.

Nevertheless, if Evita was a ruthless woman, her followers were now looking up to her as the true Saint Evita and could not keep her name from their lips. Señor A.F. Cafeiro, a junior minister in Perón's government, was of the opinion that Evita's greatest tactic was the way she actually mixed with the people, even going out into the streets to shake their hands and kiss their babies and give them pesos. He says:

Eva had no ideological formation. Perón spoke to the people from the balconies of the government house; she spoke to the people in the hospitals, in the schools. She was a revolutionary. She had no ideological idea . . . she did it in the facts. In a way she was a myth. She created a character, but she lived that character; she lived it sincerely. As a person she had also a strong personality . . . people loved her or hated her.

The people who most hated here were the people she most hated: the Oligarchs, the wealthy ('Shall we

102

burn down the Barrio Norte?' she would shriek at the crowds of *descamisados*. 'Shall I give you fire?'), particularly the women who, in the safety of their *porteno* drawing rooms, would talk about the 'little whore', about her ridiculous Social Aid Foundation, about how she had destroyed the Sociedad de Beneficencia and now dispensed all the charity whilst flaunting her own illicitly acquired riches.

Clearly they had a point. Evita's hypocrisy was blatant. Only the rich could have eyes and ears close enough to the Social Aid Foundation to know what was happening to the contributions. It was the rich who knew that Evita had a Swiss bank account, that she had a warehouse in Buenos Aires bulging with fashionable clothes, that, while she built wastefully expensive (and often useless) homes for indigent mothers and working girls, she was also one of the country's biggest property holders and the boss of six Buenos Aires newspapers, the radio station El Mundo, and at least two manufacturing plants.

'Suffer little children to come unto me,' Evita had proclaimed publicly – again comparing herself to Christ – and, while the worshipful *descamisados* were repeatedly informed of her ridiculous Children's Village (a compound of small-scale houses, a church, bank, school, jail, luxurious dormitories, dining rooms, playrooms and accommodation for hundreds of children), yes, while the *descamisados* were being reduced to tears by the saintliness of this offering, only the wealthy knew that Evita was spending more than $40,000 per annum on her wardrobe, that she shared five luxurious homes with Perón, that she gave power and wealth to the other members of her bastard family and that, most damning of all, the numerous properties she had acquired had been bought as 'investments' from some of the millions of pesos pouring into her Social Aid Foundation.

Yet Evita got away with it. She poured out her love. On the radio, on posters, on the many billboards of the city, this great love of Evita's was advertised. When Evita walked through the streets of the city, her most fanatical admirers would strew roses for her to walk on and then throw themselves onto their knees when she passed. Women would kiss her hands and weep. Men would bow their heads and tremble. They would doubtless have read, or have heard on the radio, about the infinite humility of their *Santa* Evita: about how she tended the poor, about how she suffered the sick, about how she rose at dawn and never slept before the morning hours, working herself to exhaustion for her beloved people. Her glittering jewels would not offend them. Her mink stoles would simply dazzle them. For indeed, were not these riches a true and honest sign of what the poor would one day have for themselves? Most certainly, they loved Evita. She was at heart a *descamisado*. Had they not read in her newspapers or been informed by her radio stations of how cruelly austere her childhood had been? Of how she would cook her own *empanadas* in her own old-fashioned oven and serve visitors with humble *maté*. Evita came from the farm. She was one of the poor. She wore the splendour of the Oligarchs as a sign of what would soon come to the *descamisados*. *Santa* Evita! *La Dama de la Esperanza*! Little Eva, Saint Evita, was irresistible.

Then, of course, there was how she looked. Her beauty denied all evil. First a chubby-faced girl, then a coldly seductive Lana Turner, she now possessed the pale, austere beauty of a heavily burdened, deeply responsible Grace Kelly. There is dignity to her face, yet her crimson lips hint at carnality. The carnality and the dignity combined turn her into a common dream. Those lips had to know fellatio. (So say the gauchos with admiration.) Those dark eyes had to know what suffering meant. (So sob the wives of the gauchos.) Thus her beauty speaks to all and bridges two worlds. On the one hand is the flesh that learnt its lessons in the Avenida Corrientes where a starlet must find fame on her back; on the other is that nobility, that transcendent, outpouring love that turns the most sinful woman into a saint. Evita was now a saint. She had paid her dues and emerged triumphant. She was every poor farm girl, every struggling *descamisado*'s daughter, who had struggled from obscurity to success. The Argentinians admired that.

She was by any standards a very extraordinary woman [says Sir John Balfour]. If you think of Argentina, and indeed Latin America, as a man-dominated part of the world, there was this woman who was playing a very great role; and of course she aroused very different feelings in the people with whom she lived. The Oligarchs, as she called the well-to-do and privileged people, hated her; they looked upon her as a ruthless adventuress. The masses of people, on the other hand – at any rate for a large part of the time I was there – worshipped her. They looked upon her as a lady bountiful who was disposing from Heaven.

Indeed, the *descamisados* had a good reason to love

la Dama de la Esperanza. She had defeated the Oligarchy, brought the employers to heel, and raised immeasurably the living standards of the workers. For this the Argentine males could only love her. As for the long-suppressed Argentinian women, Evita had given them the right to vote, put through an amendment whereby they would not have to show their ages on the registration polls, set up homes for unmarried working girls, and stimulated the idea of women in careers – all this in a country where women had never had a role before. In doing this she had altered for all time the balance between the sexes in Argentina and throughout Latin America.

She also gathered further massive support for herself. In fact, so strong was the additional support of the mass of women of Argentina that some, including Perón, felt that if Perón were to die, a popular vote of all Argentine men *and* women would ensure Evita's succession to the Presidency.

Santa Evita was now more popular than Juan Perón.

Chapter Thirteen

Evita's popularity was bought at the expense of the whole country's economy. During Perón's first year as President, he and Evita had managed to spend the whole of Argentina's war profits from meat, wheat and maize as well as running the country into a £500 million debt. Since then, there had been nothing but further reckless spending. During the next three years another £250 million in assets in the US were squandered and £180 million in gold in the Central Bank vaults had been reduced to a mere twenty million. Increasing the debts was the fact that the railways taken over from the British in 1948 were losing money at the rate of £50 million a year and that the huge telephone system bought from the Americans in 1946 for £22 million was losing at the rate of £9 million a year. US firms engaged in the meat-packing industry, previously one of the most prosperous in Argentina, were nearly bankrupt. Many other foreign businesses had been forced to close, including branch plants of the American Ford and General Motors companies. Inflation was rampant. The value of the peso had been halved. Money was pouring from the printing presses, the granaries were full of unsold maize, and £20 million sterling of linseed oil just could not be sold. In a desperate attempt to save the worsening situation, Perón had sacked Miguel Miranda and appointed three young men, all under forty, to restore some semblance of order out of the chaos into which the Argentine economy had sunk.

While much of the blame for this can be laid at the doorstep of the grafting and inefficient officials surrounding the equally grafting and inefficient Perón, undoubtedly a lot of it was due to Evita and her extravagant attempts to buy popularity – and this was starting to backfire on her in other ways. Government officials and military officers were resentful of Evita's constant interference in their affairs and very worried by the fact that she had usurped her husband's position and was surreptitiously running the whole country. Their attitude was probably best summed up by the opposition who, during the 1948 debate that resulted in the expulsion of the Radical Party Deputy Ernesto Sammartino for criticising Perón, said that they would not 'dance to the tune of Madame Pampadour' and charged the majority party with taking orders in the form of 'perfumed notes from the boudoir'. They were also aware that Evita, in a bid to strengthen her own position, had put her dissolute brother Juan Duarte into a top post in Perón's Secretariat; had made her eldest sister Elisa practically the political boss of Junin Province; had given the husbands of her other two sisters lucrative political appointments; and had, until Perón replaced them both, made her mother's old friend Enrique Nicolini head of the vital Posts, Telegraphs and Radio Department and given another old friend, the incompetent Miguel Miranda, the job of sorting out the whole economy.

For many, the fact that Perón had actually replaced both these old friends of Evita's was a sign that a rift was growing between them. It was felt that the famous lovers were not only creating their own overlapping administrations but were secretly fighting it out with each other in a battle for control of the strongest, most powerful country in Latin America. While this may or may not have been true, Perón's fellow party members and senior army officers were worried because, where power had made Perón more cautious, it had made Evita even more reckless.

'All or nothing was her motto', Evita had told her intimates, echoing Adolf Hitler. 'And if I go down, look out for the crash. There won't be anybody left standing.'

A further worry to the army officers – who were increasingly looking upon Perón as a deluded victim of Evita's wiles – was that in the division of authority Evita had managed to secure a decided advantage by taking control of what the Argentinians could publicly read, hear, see and, therefore, think. Newspapers and radio were now under her personal control. The Argentine film industry, largest in the Spanish-speaking world, had to submit every script for her approval, as did the theatre. Against this blanket control of, and attention given to, the public, Perón was beginning to seem relatively nebulous. Indeed, cultivating an air of Olympian detachment, he was moving farther away from the daily chores of running the country and letting Evita follow through his decisions. How much these decisions were his own and how much born from Evita's prompting was another question that haunted the military.

It was the belief of the army officers that many of Argentina's current problems had come about because Evita's activities offended tradition, made too many enemies, and were ultimately undermining the Perón government. The army was also firmly convinced that Evita was at the centre of the anti-US feelings that were currently prevalent, at a time when the Argentine needed US friendship and help. And the senior army officers, all traditionalists, as Perón had been, felt that Evita, an ambitious commoner, was antipathetic to all that they stood for.

As far as the army was concerned, Evita had traded on sex appeal, cheap emotionalism and patriotic jingoism to back her intuitive but often wayward emotional flair. It was also felt by her more nervous opponents that Evita could 'out-talk, outcoax and outmanoeuvre' Perón, and that she was gradually bewitching him into ruination.

Such fears sprang directly from the differences between Perón and *campañera* Evita. Perón, a military strategist, liked to plan each detail; Evita acted on the spur of the moment. Perón, a born politician, would pragmatically make peace with former enemies if he felt that it would benefit the government; Evita, on the other hand, a mere woman of the streets, could never forgive anyone who had ever snubbed or crossed her, no matter the cost to the government.

Clearly these differences were crucial and, in the eyes of the army officers, gradually leading to the fall of the country. They were all too aware of the fact that, while Perón had been willing to cooperate with the US for the good of Argentina, Evita was against it on the simple, childish principle that Hollywood had rejected her as a movie actress. It was also noted that Evita, still raging over her rejection by Buckingham Palace during her Rainbow Tour, had encouraged the Argentine men-of-war to dispute the Antarctic territories with Britain. She had also encouraged her servile friend Miguel Miranda to raise the price of Britain's beef to intolerable levels when Perón, who feared the dislocation of his country's traditional economy, had wanted a truce in the Antarctic tussle.

The fact that Perón had finally replaced both Miguel Miranda and Evita's Enrique Nicolini with his own men was a sign to the army that he was at least worried about Evita overreaching herself. Yet the army remained anxious because it believed that, while Perón was still motivated by deeply rooted, totalitarian convictions (acquired through the army and his admiration for Mussolini), plus a desire for a place in history as Argentina's Man of Destiny, Evita was driven by more elemental, therefore destructive, urges: the desire for respectability, wealth, absolute power and, clearly, revenge.

The army finally became convinced of Evita's insatiable lust for power and of Perón's gradual domination by her when, in early 1951, he suggested that she be put up as a candidate for the Vice-Presidency.

By now, Perón, fifty-three years of age, was looking ill and exhausted, his face blotched by eczema, and he was smoking two packets of cigarettes a day. Evita, on the other hand, had never been so relentless in pursuing what she wanted and seemed illuminated from within by the flame of her own burning ambition. To the army, therefore, this latest announcement by Perón was a sign that Evita had to be stopped.

(It is worth noting at this juncture that to the army the very thought of a woman Vice-President was abhorrent and ran counter to the whole history and tradition of the Argentine. It is also worth pointing out that even if Evita had been an exemplary and honest political figure – which she was not – the very fact that she was a woman would have ensured the army's firm resistance. Argentina was a *man's* country and Evita's liberation of women was something for which the army, the seat of tradition, would never forgive her.)

Evita's plan, which was to seek out the Vice-Presidency in the 1952 election on the ticket with Perón, was based on the fact that of Perón's three main sources of power – the Women's Party, the General Confederation of Labour, and the Peronists – the last was the weakest in voting power while the first two were now directly controlled by herself. In fact, it was Evita's public identification with the mass of Argentine women that had immeasurably strengthened her position and made her stronger than Perón.

> I am only a humble woman belonging to a vast nation . . . A woman the same as millions of others in the world. God chose me and put me here, beside the leader of the world: Perón. Why was I chosen and not someone else? I don't know. I only think of myself as the humble representative of the women in the country. I feel that, like them, I am at the heart of a home . . . the fortune home that is my Fatherland which Perón is leading to its highest peak of fulfilment . . . Within the great home of the Fatherland, I am exactly the same as any other woman in any of the numerous homes in our nation. Like her, I am, in the final reckoning, a woman.

An early sign of the Vice-Presidency bid was when, following Evita's visit to Perón with the leaders of the Women's Party, the President, in naming the Women's Party, the General Confederation of Labour and the Peronists as his three major assets, had pointedly omitted any reference to the army, which he was supposed to represent. This was immediately noted by political observers and interpreted, correctly, as an open invitation to nominate Evita for the Vice-Presidential candidacy.

Evita's savage ruthlessness had grown in direct proportion to her reputation as a saint and nowhere was this more evident than in her attempts to clear the decks of all possible rivals to herself for the Vice-Presidency.

The first victim was Colonel Juan Mercante, an old friend of Perón's and a man who, as Governor of the Province of Buenos Aires, was entitled to regard himself as the natural successor to the Vice-President. One evening, when the colonel was en route from La Plata to Buenos Aires in answer to a summons from Perón, his car had a collision with a hit-and-run driver. Mercante, who was lucky to have escaped with his life, emerged from the 'accident' a very frightened man. Shortly afterwards, he announced that he would not be standing for the Vice-Presidency.

Another possible contender was Colonel Filomeno Velazco, Chief of Federal Police. Strangely, after announcing that he was going to run in the forthcoming elections, he, like Colonel Mercante, received a call from President Perón, summoning him to come to Buenos Aires for an unspecified purpose. Aware of what had happened to Colonel Mercante, Velazco pleaded illness, remained in Corrientes Province, and displayed no further ambitions regarding the Vice-Presidency.

With the competition removed from the political arena, Evita now swung her massive propaganda machinery into action. Apart from the usual election-eering tactics, such as supporters wearing shirts and pullovers inscribed with 'Perón Achieves!' and 'Evita Dignifies!', other supporters involving themselves in highly publicised competitions and stunts, and the Evita-controlled radio and press pouring out their customary lies, Evita also sank to offering bicycles, dolls and other toys to children as an inducement to their parents to visit the capital for demonstrations in a Buenos Aires park. So great were the crowds that many did not get to within a quarter-mile of the park, thousands returned home with wet eyes and empty hands, and beneath the huge banners emblazoned with 'Suffer little children to come unto me', two children were knocked down and trampled to death. Evita also reverted to her 1945 trick of supplying free transport, food and drink to encourage thousands more to her demonstrations. (All opposition attempts to do the same were blocked.) Last but by no means least, the new edition of Argentina's *Who's Who*, in a biography dictated by the thirty-two-year-old Evita, gave her age as twenty-nine – a year less than the age set by the constitution for candidates for the Vice-Presidency. In the event, Evita's combination of vanity and cunning contributed to her first major disaster.

As an inducement for a popular demonstration for her nomination on 22 August 1951, Evita had planned to gather together at least two and a half million supporters in the vast Plaza Moreno on Avenida 9 de Julio, most of whom were to be drilled in shouting and pleading for her to accept the Vice-Presidency. Timed to run from Thursday morning to Saturday night, the spectacular show turned out to be a spectacular disaster.

Earlier that week, the opposition learned of Evita's false entry in the Argentine *Who's Who* and used it to publicly flay her and make a fool of her, either castigating her for blatant dishonesty or making jokes about her 'feminine' vanity. They also made it clear that the army had refused to accept her nomination. The ploy worked. Evita's popularity had already been waning because of the punitive measures she had introduced in order to bolster up an economy being drained by her own 'charitable' enterprises. Realising that they were now being made to pay for the many benefits that she had given them, the *descamisados* were beginning to wonder where it all might end. Thus, when they learned that Evita had lied about her age and, also, that the army was now resolutely against her, they failed to give her the support she had expected.

Only one-tenth of the anticipated number turned out for the meeting in the Plaza Moreno and most of the few who came did not even stay long enough to hear Evita stumbling through the farce of 'bowing to the will of the people' and accepting the nomination. The planned three-day fiesta had to be cancelled, Evita abruptly fled from the Plaza, the scene of her humiliation, and within hours there was widespread speculation that she might not run at all.

This was true. Shocked by the knowledge of her diminishing popularity, humiliated that her real age had been revealed by the opposition, and finally thwarted by the army's refusal to accept her nomination, Evita was forced to accept her first defeat.

On 2 September, eleven days after the nightmarish affair, Evita, dressed in a severe black suit and a high-necked black blouse, spoke on the radio, her voice trembling and hoarse, torn by the barbs of its own dishonesty:

> I want to communicate an irrevocable and definite decision to my people, a decision I have taken by myself, to resign the noted honour given to me by the open forum of the twenty-second. Already, on that memorable afternoon, I realised that I should not change the post I already held with the Peronist movement for any other. I have only one great personal ambition; that is, when history writes its glorious chapter on Perón, for it to be said in a small footnote: 'Beside him was a woman who dedicated her whole time to expressing the hopes of the people to General Perón, who then converted them into reality, and that this woman was known, caressingly, as Evita.'

And Evita was dying.

Chapter Fourteen

In January 1951, when Evita was operated on for appendicitis, the surgeons had seen what they suspected was the beginning of cancer. Later, during that fateful September, Evita's Secretariat announced that she was suffering from 'influenza'. Later still, it was announced that she was to be operated on for 'pernicious anaemia', an illness for which there is no known operation. What was *not* announced was that in October Dr Abel Carcano, the leading Argentine cancer specialist, flew to Evita's despised United States of America to bring back Dr George Pack, famed cancer surgeon of New York's Memorial Hospital. On 4 November, after examination by Dr Pack, Evita was admitted to the Polyclinico Presidente Perón, and, two days later, news bulletins announced that she'd had surgery for the removal of a uterine growth.

In fact, she was dying from cancer of the uterus, haemorrhaging through the vagina, and already starting to waste away.

The waning of Evita's popularity was obviously tied to the waning of the country's economic stability. Yet, if the healthy have faults, the dying rest in renewed purity and the news of Evita's illness would give her back her lost credibility. Over the past eight years, Evita had made many enemies and their dissatisfaction with her had recently spread even to her beloved *descamisados*. What had once been only rumours and gossip about her Social Aid Foundation extravagances had turned into hard facts and much grumbling was going on amongst the 'shirtless ones'. Perhaps sensing this, Evita had long since dropped her flamboyant manner of dress and started appearing in more simple clothes, her long blonde hair pulled back tight around her sharp features to lend her a rather maternal look.

When her blatantly propagandist, autobiographical book, *La Razon di mi Vida* (*The Reason for my Life*), was published that year, it contained more than a dozen photographs of Evita in her jewels and grossly expensive clothes; yet once the book was issued Evita, clearly realising that this was no longer the politically correct image, had the first edition withdrawn and a new edition published, with the original photos removed and the new ones showing her in dark, severe suits, moving about in the homes, shops and factories of the workers. This gesture, however, came too late. Well before her disastrous bid for the Vice-Presidency, crude posters had begun to appear on the billboards of Buenos Aires depicting her standing nude with crowds of little men marching between her legs – a reminder of her past as a 'little whore', of her megalomaniacal ambitions, and of the fact that even the *descamisados* were becoming disillusioned.

Amongst the items that had led to the waning of Evita's once shining image was the fact that increasingly she had become exposed as Perón's hatchet woman. If Perón wanted someone removed from the political scene (or from the streets), it was Evita who arranged to have it done. Indeed, in Uruguay, the customary first stop for the exiles who got away alive from Perón's dangerous Argentina, Evita was now known as 'Pocahontas' for her acknowledged ability with the tomahawk. This image, which contrasted violently with Evita's other image as saint, was compounded by the massive expansion of Perón's Secret Service and by the increasing number of accusations of torture by members of his staff.

Lisandfo Saldivar, one of the highest-paid members of Evita's Ministry of Labour and Welfare, was tried and, naturally, acquitted three times of charges of homicide. Martinez, the Chief of Police, who had been denounced by US Ambassador Spruille Braden, was accused by the exiled author Ernesto Sammartino of torturing to death Carlos Aguirre, friend of the leading union man Cipriano Reyes; Sammartino added that Reyes himself (once a Perón ally) had become a mere wreck of a man as the result of torture he had undergone repeatedly in a Peronist prison after he had shown 'disrespect' to Perón. And, since Evita covered up and protected her husband from such charges, her own reputation was greatly tainted.

Another black mark against Evita – even apart from the growing rumours of deliberate mishandling of the Foundation's funds – was her penchant for looking after her relatives at the expense of the country. After Evita's succession to power, her sister Elisa, who had no political or administrative experience of any kind, was made political boss of the Province of Junin; while her husband, Alfredo Arrieta, rose quickly from nowhere to become a member of the Argentine Senate. Dr Justo Rodriguez, husband to another of Evita's sisters, Blanca, was highly publicised by the Eva Perón Publicity Office as the 'coming' judge of the Argentine courts and eventually became Minister of the Supreme Court of Argentina. Orlando Bertolini, whose only experience in politics was in operating the lift in the Town Hall of Vincente Lopez, married Evita's other sister, Erminda, and quickly became a director of both Argentine's Customs Department and the government-operated fishing company, the Maritime Hunt. Finally, and most deplorable of all, Evita continued to protect, when not actually encouraging, her dissolute brother, Juan, and his many criminal activities. Noted especially at the time was the receipt of £1,150,000 from some Italian businessmen in return for letting them bring an aluminium factory into Argentina (Juan was placed temporarily under house arrest, but subsequently released) and the alleged favouritism shown in the granting of import licences to certain US firms in return for considerable sums of money.

Nevertheless, with the news of Evita's illness, a wave of love and sympathy swept the nation. Much of this was due to the religious romanticism of the Argentinians, to the fact that they could no longer think of Evita as anyone other than *Santa* Evita, and to the fact that Evita had, over the past year, been displaying an extraordinary, passionate and emotion-arousing conviction about the glory of the Peróns and Argentina.

Some time between 1947 and 1949, Evita started believing her own propaganda. Certainly, as early as 1947 she was publicly comparing her husband to Caesar, Alexander the Great and Napoleon. In fact, her fervour was such that she could later write without a trace of irony: 'Nobody, absolutely nobody in the course of history has received such delirious affection from their people as Perón has done . . . If anyone has, then no one has known how to use it for the happiness of their people, as he has.'

120

By 1949 her delusions of grandeur had turned into religious conviction and she was telling a meeting of newly enfranchised women political leaders of Argentina that it would not surprise her if one day they should 'wake up to find that Perón has disappeared from the earth, and thus the Divine Visitation will be over.' Increasingly convinced that Perón's spiritual stature (therefore her own) was positively godlike, she was soon implying, by way of soothing the troubled Catholic Church, that if Perón was not a God he was at least guided by 'Holy Inspiration'. Statements of this kind became commonplace until, her deluded dreams getting the better of her, at a huge demonstration in the Buenos Aires football stadium, she blasphemed in the eyes of the church with a particularly melodramatic piece of rhetoric.

'Perón is the air we breathe!' she shrieked into her microphone. 'Perón is our sun! Perón is our life! The humble people, my General, have come here to prove, as they have always done, that the miracle which happened two thousand years ago is occurring again!'

Fantasy and fact were now one and indivisible. The character she had created was taking her over and she, a failed actress, was now playing the role of her life.

'The role of Eva Perón seems easy to me,' she wrote. 'And that's not surprising. Isn't it always much easier to play a theatrical role than to live it in reality? I'm quite sure that in my case, as Eva Perón, I'm playing a traditional role which many women have played throughout the years.'

So much for Little Eva, the housewife. As for Evita, the beloved *Santa* Evita: 'As Evita, I'm living out a reality which perhaps no other woman has experienced in the history of humanity.'

Yes, in discarding the Christian Dior gowns and mink sables and diamonds, in wearing the clothes of a plain woman and binding her blonde hair behind her head like a matron, she was not becoming modest or accepting her age, but was, instead, displaying a growing infatuation with herself – or with that image of herself as a saint bringing God to the people. If Perón was God, Evita sat at his right hand, the living link between Him and His shirtless ones, the heart and soul of the country.

I shall never forget that I was once, and that I still am, a swallow. If I fly higher, it's thanks to him. If I move among the clouds, it's thanks to him. If my wings sometimes almost touch Heaven, it's thanks to him. If I see clearly who my people are, and if I love them and feel their affection caressing my name, it is only through him . . . I held the lamp that lighted his darkness; I kept it burning as best I knew how, guarding his flank with my love and his faith.

To the *descamisados* such sentiments had been irresistible and now, with the news of Evita's mortal illness, they would return to consume them. In that bleak year of 1952, while Evita lay on her sickbed, as she haemorrhaged from the vagina and the flesh shrank on her bones, the lost love of the shirtless ones welled up again and they were blinded by grief. Now the billboards in Buenos Aires, which had formerly shown a crimson-lipped Eva, the smiling star of their collective dreams, were displaying a new Evita, a more spiritual, austere beauty: her blonde hair pulled tight behind her small head; her face pale, almost ethereal; her lips now unpainted; her brown eyes imbued with tragic understanding, gazing down forgivingly on her flock.

Doubtless she had trouble believing in the reality of it – was driven to believe that she could defeat the growing cancer and live on to fight another day. For indeed, how could she die? Her work was not finished yet. Touched by glory and the conviction of her own eternal worth, she would not be able to accept that it must finally end.

Thus she continued working. She worked less, but she kept going. She made occasional forays into the harsh light of day, looking wasted and pale and slightly haunted, to talk, or croak, to her people, then she was carried back to her dark room and wrapped up in her bed, racked by pain and exhausted. Still she would not accept it. It could not be happening to her. Had she not come from obscurity, from ignorance and humiliation, to climb to the unassailable heights, to be supreme, inviolable?

Until I die [she wrote] I want to be able to open new horizons and paths to my poor people, my workers, and to my women. I know that, like any other woman, I am stronger than I seem, and am healthier than the doctors believe. Like them, I am prepared to continue struggling for happiness at home. I am not aiming at anything other than this happiness! This is my vocation and my destiny. This is my mission. Like any other woman in the country, I want to fulfil it right up to the end. Perhaps one day, when I am definitely dying . . .

But dying she was. Her draining blood told the tale. She was finally compelled to stay in her bed and vote for Perón from there. After this, she had no choice. She simply had to accept it. She was drugged and yet the pain would not leave her; it bit and it tore. Doubtless, her religion helped her. She was still a practising Catholic. She had God on the one hand and her 'shirtless ones' on the other, and she would live on as *Santa* Evita, the sanctified myth. She believed in it wholly now. It was probably what sustained her. With her dark eyes burning out of that frightening skeleton's head, she perceived a world kneeling in worship to her own blinding image . . . Little Eva. Evita. *Santa* Evita . . . She wept for joy and was comforted.

How did Evita die? Reportedly with great courage. It was the courage of a growing, megalomaniacal belief in her own spiritual affinity with Argentina. Not for nothing had the people said that in bedding down with Perón, Evita had been bedding down with the whole nation. It had been suggested that she was sexless, that her orgasms were found in power, that her love affair with Perón was a love affair with the whole of the Argentine. Now Evita was proving it – broadcasting from her deathbed. As her face shrank, her brown eyes grew enormous and held a fierce luminosity.

'Today,' she had said in October 1951, 'I have left my sickbed to pay a debt of gratitude to Perón and to the workers. I do not care if I have to part with pieces of my life to pay for it.'

Who could resist such a performance? Her death could only ennoble her. And, if she had been ill in October, she was much worse the following year, in

June 1952, when Perón was sworn in as President for the second time. Could Evita disappoint her subjects? Was she not a bridge from them to Perón? So now Evita had to go on to reaffirm her own sanctity, to appear before the public for the very last time, and she did so heavily sedated, looking no more than a wraith. She fainted twice and was then carried away and was not seen again.

In the final month of Evita's life, which was spent entirely in her sickroom, Argentina scrambled to pour new honours upon her. While hearing fifty-nine speeches of eulogy, Congress officially made her 'Spiritual Chief of the Nation', ordered the construction of a huge monument in downtown Buenos Aires, and conferred on her the 753-diamond Collar of the Order of the Liberator. Prayers for her recovery were said day and night. However, a series of crises carried her lower and lower, until, towards the end, she weighed less than eighty pounds. 'I am too little for so much pain!' she cried. Finally, when ever larger injections of morphine threatened to kill her, surgeons severed some brain nerves to reduce the pain. Meanwhile, Peronist fanaticism reached such a pitch that sobbing women crawled repeatedly around the Presidential mansion on their hands and knees.

On 9 July 1952, President Perón hurried away from the Independence Day parade, refusing to remain for the scheduled ceremony of lowering the flag, in order to be by the bedside of his dying wife. Ten days later, at 6.30 p.m., the government's Bureau of Information interrupted radio programmes on all Argentine stations to broadcast a bulletin which said: 'The state of health of Señora Perón declined noticeably this afternoon.' Police cordons were thrown around the

President's residence and traffic was detoured within two blocks of the house. Finally, on 26 July at 9.42 p.m., all radio stations interrupted their programmes to report: 'The Sub-Secretariat of Information fulfils the very sad duty of announcing that at 8.25 o'clock, Señora Eva Perón, the Spiritual Chief of the Nation, passed away.' The announcement was followed by religious music.

At the bedside when Evita died were President Perón and a dozen relatives and close friends, including her mother, Señora Juana Ibarguren de Duarte; her three sisters, Elisa Duarte de Arrieta, Blanca Duarte de Alvarez and Erminda Duarte de Bertolini; her brother Juan Duarte; the Governor of Buenos Aires, Carlos Aloe; Minister of Communications, Oscar Nicolini; Minister of Technical Affairs, Raul Mendez; Minister of Political Affairs, Ramon Subiza; the Under-Secretary of Press, Raul Apold; and Señora Perón's personal secretary, Atilio Renzi.

Outside the residence, thousands of *descamisados* had gathered to resurrect and deify the legend of Evita.

She had died at the age of thirty-three

Part Three

RESURRECTION AND IMMORTALITY

Suffer little children to come unto me.

— Evita

Chapter Fifteen

On 2 September 1971, a hearse belonging to an Italian undertaker's firm left Milan for Madrid. The funeral company had been contracted to transport to Spain the body of a woman. According to her documents she was Maria Maggi de Magistris, born in Dalmine, Italy, died in Rosario, Argentina, 23 February 1951.

The contract had been drawn up by a man who said he was the dead woman's brother, Carlos, and that he was carrying out his mother's last wish to have the body buried with her in a grave in Madrid. The driver's name was Roberto Germani and only much later did he discover whose body he had actually transported to Madrid.

With Carlos Maggi (actually the Argentine intelligence officer, Hector Cabanillas) beside him, Germani headed for the French border. Since the Argentine authorities had secured the cooperation of the Italian, French and Spanish governments, there were no searches or delays at customs posts. However, once inside France the hearse was escorted by motorised *gendarmes* as it raced towards Spain. The hearse spent one night in a Perpignan garage, then early next morning it was driven across the Spanish frontier, where it was escorted by two carloads of Spanish police on the final 460-mile lap to Madrid.

The cavalcade drove to the Calle de Navalmanzano

in Madrid's most elegant suburb, Puerta de Hierro, and stopped at number six, a two-and-a-half-storey, gabled house of modern design, standing in spacious grounds behind a screen of tall cypress trees. Parked outside, as it was every day and night, was a jeep crammed with uniformed policemen. Two plain-clothes policemen of the political brigade, both wearing dark glasses, strolled up and down the pavement in front of the house.

Waiting on the steps were the 70-year-old Juan Perón, his 39-year-old wife, Isabel, secretary Lopez Rega, Perón's personal representative, Jorge Paladino, and Brigadier Jorge Rojas Silveyra, Ambassador in Madrid.

Under the watchful eyes of the security men, the coffin was removed from the hearse, carried into the house, placed on the dining-room table and then, in an 'eerie silence', prised open.

'I went three times to look at Evita,' Perón had written fifteen years previously. 'The doors . . . were like the gates of eternity.'

Now, standing beside his third wife, Isabel (not counting the reported marriage to 19-year-old Laura de Solar), and gazing down at the face he had not seen for so long, Juan Domingo Perón openly wept.

'She is not dead,' he said of Evita. 'She is sleeping – only sleeping!'

The body was quickly removed to a basement room where, the following Sunday, it was examined by Dr Pedro Ara, the eminent pathologist and mortician who had originally embalmed it. Dr Ara, a small, bald, Spaniard who travelled with the guillotined head of a creole beggar in his baggage, was much in demand with the aristocracy for his skill at transforming the dead into 'permanent sculptures'. Reportedly, he had studied the extraordinary embalming process employed on Lenin and had, for a reported fee of £100,000, taken a year doing the same to Evita.

First, he had replaced her blood with alcohol, later with glycerine of a temperature of sixty degrees Celsius, pumped in through the heel and an ear. Reduced to normal temperature, the glycerine solidified, leaving the body semi-embalmed, its organs and skin intact, the skin now having an unusual elasticity. Finally, the body was dehydrated and immersed in unspecified chemicals. After a year the skin took on a near transparency, a pale, tranquil beauty, though the corpse itself had been reduced in size to that of a twelve-year-old girl.

Examination of the corpse now revealed that both knees had been broken; the chest was marked with half a dozen perforations and a wide cut near the throat; the nose was broken; cuts were visible on the left ribs, forehead and left cheek. Evita's blonde hair had been cut off at the neck and her shroud was in tatters.

Washed, repaired and clad in a fresh white shroud sewn by Evita's sisters, Elisa and Blanca, the body was placed in a new blue-silk-lined oak coffin. According to unsubstantiated reports, Perón kept the coffin on the dining table for many months in order to weep over the corpse every day. More likely is that the coffin was taken upstairs, where it was securely locked up in a small room under the eaves. There it was to remain until the people called Perón back to the Argentine.

Evita had been missing for seventeen years.

Chapter Sixteen

When, in 1955, the revolution had driven Perón into exile, his immediate successor, General Lonardi, realised that possession of Evita's body by one or other of the rival factions could become an inflammatory issue. The deposed Perón, now plotting relentlessly in Madrid, had begun making demands to have Evita's body shipped to him; but the new President, obviously playing for time, refused all such requests, also refused the Duarte family, and deliberately appointed a government team to 'determine the authenticity' of the corpse. A thumb was duly amputated and its prints examined. Evita's identity was confirmed. Further requests from the distant Juan Perón were pointedly ignored.

On 19 November, a mere four months after he had taken office, General Lonardi was ousted by General Pedro Aramburu and Evita was kidnapped from her resting place in Room 63 in CGT headquarters in the Calle Azopardo. In command of this operation was Colonel Carlos Eugenio de Moori Koenig, head of military intelligence and a bitter enemy of Perón, who had previously demoted him. Also in the room at the time was the pathologist and mortician, Dr Ara, who had been making one of his regular inspections of the corpse. Unable to challenge the authority of Colonel Koenig, nor that of the armed soldiers around him, Dr Ara had no choice but to let them remove the body to 'ensure that it gets a decent burial'. Subsequently, the corpse was dumped in a cut-price coffin, slung into the back of an army truck, and driven off into the night.

The body was taken to a warehouse near Military Intelligence headquarters where it stayed for a further two months, its whereabouts kept secret. Then, on 5 January 1956, it was moved again, first to one place, then to another, until eventually, after five stops, it was transferred to a packing case and delivered to the apartment of Koenig's deputy, Major Antonio Arandia.

Evita's influence, even in death, proved destructive again.

News of the 'kidnapping' and subsequent disappearance of Evita's body had aroused faithful Peronists to a howling fury. As wild rumours swept the country (Evita had been cremated; her body had been thrown into the River Plata; it had been stolen by Perón and was presently with him in Uruguay; it was in the crypts of the Duarte or Perón families), the Peronists searched through Buenos Aires, scouring the streets for news of Evita's whereabouts.

As many of the more fanatical Peronists were armed, Major Arandia took to sleeping with a pistol under his pillow. One night, disturbed by strange noises and not knowing that his pregnant wife had gone to the bathroom, he saw a shadow in the bedroom doorway, fired twice and killed his wife outright.

Major Arandia's wife was duly buried and Evita was moved once more, this time to the fourth floor of the Military Intelligence headquarters. Still in the packing crate, she was stacked amongst other packing crates, all labelled as holding radio sets, and left there while Koenig flew off to Chile to propose handing over the body to Evita's mother.

This plan did not go through. In June, Koenig was replaced by the head of President Aramburu's Secret Service, Colonel Hector Cabanillas, who soon discovered the packing crate on the fourth floor. Informing President Aramburu of this, he was told by the President to arrange a Christian burial.

As Evita's presence in the capital might further inflame the Peronists, Colonel Cabanillas decided against burying her there. Instead, he had a lot of identical coffins made. One of these contained Evita's corpse; the others were filled with lead the weight of a medium-sized woman. (According to an Argentine bestselling *roman-à-clef*, *Santa Evita*, by Tomas Eloy Martinez, the coffins contained several identical replicas of the corpse, sculpted from wax and vinyl. However, no proof for this claim has been offered and it seems highly unlikely.) That September, the various coffins were taken from Argentina by plane and by ship, each coffin bound for a different destination and each courier convinced that he alone was about to bury the real Evita. Each of the coffins was duly buried while the real Evita was shipped to Bonn via Brussels. In Bonn, unknown to Ambassador Raoul de Labugle, it was stored for some months with the dead files and bric-a-brac in the Embassy storeroom. From there it went eventually, via Rome, to Milan.

When the body arrived in Milan, it was in the care of Giuseppina Airoldia, a lay sister of the Society of St Paul. The sister had been told that the body was that of Maria Maggi de Magistris, an Italian widow who had died in Argentina with a last request to be interred in her homeland. So it was that under the name of Maria Maggi de Magistris, the corpse of Evita Perón was finally laid to rest in lot 86, garden 41 of the Musocco Cemetery in Milan.

It remained there, undisturbed, for fifteen years.

Meanwhile, as is customary with turbulent Argentina, a new President, General Alexjandro Lanusse, had assumed power. In April 1971, he announced that Evita's body should be found and returned to her ex-husband, Juan Perón. In order that this be expedited as quickly as possible, intelligence agents, policemen, priests and Perón's old associates were sent swarming across Buenos Aires, Spain and Italy, questioning innumerable people and ransacking various vaults for old documents. All of this was in vain. Eventually, for reasons still not explained, President Lanusse decided to call on his personal confessor, Father Rotger.

It transpired that Father Rotger, with the assistance of members of the Vatican, had arranged the transfer of the body to Italy. Now in hiding in Madrid because of assassination threats by the same Peronist terrorists who had, a year earlier, murdered President Aramburu, Father Rotger was persuaded to emerge from hiding and fly to Milan for a meeting with Colonel Cabanillas. After telling Cabanillas where the body of Evita was actually buried, Father Rotger returned to Madrid and Colonel Cabanillas, alias Carlos Maggi, went to the Milan cemetery armed with written permission to exhume his fictitious sister's remains.

Thus, on 3 September 1971, after a total of sixteen years, Juan Perón was reunited with Evita.

Chapter Seventeen

Evita's embalmed body had been returned to Señor Perón as a weak gesture of reconciliation by the military government in Argentina. The reason is that Perón, obsessed with returning to power in his country, had for years been controlling his loyal Peronists from his villa in the Puerta de Hierro in Madrid. Now affectionately called *El Viejo* (the old man), Perón would chainsmoke cigarettes, pore over the flood of political reports that came into the villa daily by special telex from Buenos Aires, six thousand miles away, and send commands back by the same telex. Bankrolled by the Justicialista Party in Argentina, Peronist labour unions and some wealthy sympathisers, Perón had for twelve years been able to destroy every successive government and poison every effort to restore Argentina's political and economic health. In doing so, he was hoping that Argentina's economy would continue to deteriorate and that nostalgia would then create an overwhelming urge for the Good Old Days.

Remarkably, he was correct. The many young Peronists who demonstrated in the streets of Argentina could remember little, and doubtless cared even less, about the more revolting aspects of the Perón/Evita regime seventeen years before. Rather, what they remembered was the beauty of Evita, the generosity of Perón, the love and the support that both had shown for the 'shirtless ones'. Now Argentina was in chaos once more and its economy was nearly in ruins. Forgetting the Secret Service and the arbitrary arrests, the torture and the deportations and the general corruption of the Perón era, a good third of the country still yearned for the return of Perón and the sense of grandeur that he and Evita had generated.

Gradually becoming aware of the fact that the insatiable Perón, with the aid of another young, attractive, show-business wife, was managing to disrupt the government even from faraway Madrid, President Lieutenant-General Alexjandro Lanusse, who twenty years before had been sentenced to life imprisonment by Perón, was obliged to find and return Evita's body as a sign of good will. As if this were not bad enough, Lanusse, realising that if Argentina should not be run by Perón it certainly could not be run *without* him, was forced to eat humble pie and allow Perón to revisit his home country.

The initial return of *El Viejo* was disappointing. On 18 November 1972, accompanied by dark, slim and remote Isabel, Perón stepped down from his Alitalia jet on to the tarmac of a rainswept Buenos Aires – not to the teeming thousands he had anticipated, but to a mere *three* thousand extremely wet Peronists. The lack of numbers was due to the fact that President Lanusse had cordoned off the airport for ten miles in every direction with 35,000 heavily armed troops and armoured cars and tanks. Lanusse himself had cold-shouldered the arrival; and when some two thousand Peronists tried to storm the barricades, they were driven back with guns and tear-gas.

As Perón left the airport to be grilled by Brigadier General Martinez (subsequently receiving permission to hold the first of his many rallies), sixty petty officers at a naval engineering school on the outskirts of Buenos Aires were surrounding the officers' quarters and demonstrating in favour of their former President and his enchanting Evita. After shooting two of the guards, the petty officers took four hostages and fled towards the airport, where they later surrendered.

Proof as this was that the fervour of certain Peronists had not dimmed, that fervour had not yet become the plague that would bring Perón back. After settling into his house in fashionable Vincente Lopez, Perón talked patiently and cleverly to the thousands who daily massed outside, marshalled his forces for the electoral battle scheduled to take place in February 1973, and got down to the business of laying the groundwork for a national coalition to take over from Argentina's present military rulers. However, President Lanusse slyly scotched these plans by refusing to rescind an edict requiring Presidential candidates to have been in Argentina on 25 August, thereby rendering Perón's candidacy obsolete before it even began. Shortly after, a defeated Perón returned to Madrid.

Yet Perón was not finished. Now, after eight presidents, most of them military men, Argentina, an immense and fertile country, rich in grain and cattle, with a population of twenty-three million, was drifting ever closer to chaos. The people were in despair, their pockets were empty, and they thought increasingly about Perón and Evita, who between them had sustained a vision of the country's greatness. Almost shirtless again, certainly penniless and frightened, the *descamisados* remembered Perón's strength, his bold decisiveness, and Evita's abiding hatred of the rich.

Religious, superstitious, they also thought of Evita's body, which reportedly, after twenty years, had not decomposed. And suddenly, not surprisingly, it all happened again: everyone was a Peronist.

Again the billboards of Buenos Aires featured pictures of Evita and a wave of nostalgia swept through the Argentine.

As we've seen, in the first election of 1973, Perón was unable to stand because of the residency requirements imposed by the outgoing regime. However, with Perón controlling the whole show from his villa in Madrid, his colleague Hector Campora became the standard-bearer of Peronism and was elected President with 39 per cent of the vote. This mission accomplished, on 21 June Perón flew back to Buenos Aires to repeat the Perón/Evita spectacle by preparing to run for President in the forthcoming September elections with his wife, Isabel, aiming for the Vice-Presidency.

Perón's arrival in Buenos Aires was noteworthy for the customary violence that accompanied it. The Argentine army refused a request for President Campora to increase security precautions and twenty people were killed and 380 injured when vicious gunfighting broke out at Ezeiza airport. There were no troops at the airport, there were very few police, and young Peronists were used to keep order.

Three weeks later, President Campora suddenly resigned and, in the elections of September 1973, Juan Domingo Perón was again voted in as President with his wife, Isabel, as Vice-President.

Nine months later, on 1 July 1974, President Juan Domingo Perón died at the age of seventy-eight.

Chapter Eighteen

Isabel Perón was born Maria Estela Isabel Martinez on 4 February 1931, in the province of La Rioja, north-west of Buenos Aires. She was the youngest of six children of a bank executive who died in 1938 after moving with his family to the capital.

Isabel never went beyond the sixth grade at school, but she studied the piano and dancing, appeared in folk music groups and nightclub acts, and dreamed of becoming a star.

It was when she was performing as a dancer in a nightclub in Panama that Isabel met General Juan Domingo Perón, who was in exile after the military coup that had displaced him.

Isabel was thirty-five years younger than General Perón.

Isabel became his 'companion' and secretary, answering letters and typing the manuscripts of the numerous books that the former President was then writing.

Isabel accompanied Juan Perón when he moved from Panama to Venezuela, then to the Dominican Republic, and finally to Spain where, in 1961, he married her.

Isabel Perón became the President of Argentina.

Chapter Nineteen

The funeral of General Perón was delayed while hundreds of thousands of people filed past his open coffin in the Congress Building in Buenos Aires. Such scenes of mourning had not been witnessed in the Argentine capital since the death of Evita in July 1952.

Perón had left instructions that he was not to be embalmed and that his body was to be buried in his family tomb in the cemetery of Chacarita. Instead, he was returned to the chapel of his home in the suburb of Olivos where the embalming process, already begun, was completed.

During his last nine months as President of Argentina, Perón, faced with a dangerous war between the left and right wings in his movement, had chosen the right. Subsequently, the young radicals and guerrilla groups, who had demonstrated and fought in the streets for his return, became disillusioned. However, though Perón had betrayed the left, the memory of Evita lived on. In fact, it was the disappearance of her body that had helped to keep the Peronist myth alive and fire a new generation who had come to see in Peronism those virtues that had never existed in the first place. 'Evita lives! Evita lives!' they chanted during their demonstrations. And so, beyond any shadow of doubt, it was the young revolutionary left wing's identification with the dead Evita that encouraged the new President, Isabel Perón, to bring Evita's body back to the Argentine.

In a radio and television address to the nation, announcing the return of Evita's body, Señora Perón called her 'the Spiritual Leader of the Nation'. She also said that the 'sacred' remains of Evita would lie, together with those of General Perón, in the Olivos Chapel, from where they would eventually be transferred to the Altar of the Fatherland, the mausoleum then being built in a Buenos Aires suburb.

The embalmed body of Evita was flown from Madrid to Buenos Aires on 17 November 1974. Isabel Perón, General Perón's third wife and political heir, accompanied by two of Evita's sisters, headed a large committee of government and military officials as the remains were taken by car from the airport to the presidential chapel in Olivos, on the outskirts of Buenos Aires. Thousands of men, women and children lined the route, throwing flowers at the passing car and weeping.

The embalmed body of Evita was put on public display in December 1974, in a crypt at the Presidential residence at Olivos. It lay beside the sealed coffin of General Perón.

Twenty-four years after her death, in October 1976, the body of Maria Eva Duarte de Perón was finally returned to her family. It now lies fifteen feet underground in a specially armoured private vault in the most exclusive cemetery of Buenos Aires.

Determined that the Duarte family vault in the Recoleta Cemetery should be Evita's final resting place, secure from further political body-snatching, the family and the military authorities called in a firm specialising in the construction of armoured bank vaults to reinforce the tomb.

In the centre of the floor of the burial chamber containing the coffins of other departed Duartes, an elaborate trapdoor has been inserted. It consists of three heavy-gauge steel plates, each individually locked with a different combination. The hinges are embedded in specially reinforced concrete and the cracks between the doors are covered with another thick steel flange. Beneath this hopefully impregnable trapdoor, in total darkness and eternal silence, is a second burial chamber containing the corpse, either well preserved or rotting, of Eva Perón.

'I will return,' Evita had said. 'And I will be millions.'

Part Four

*Only I can do Eva Perón. She went hungry like me,
and like me she left her home town in order to succeed.*
– Madonna

Chapter Twenty

Evita was always an unlikely subject for a musical, but Andrew Lloyd Webber, composer, and Tim Rice, lyricist, were an unlikely couple whose previous stage musical, *Jesus Christ Superstar*, had given them a taste for the big, controversial subject.

Andrew Lloyd Webber is undoubtedly a musical prodigy. Born in London on 22 March 1948, he was saturated in music from childhood. His grandfather, William Charles Henry Webber, sang with the George Mitchell Choir and the Black and White Minstrels. His father, William Southcombe Lloyd Webber, was professor of theory and musical composition at the Royal College of Music. His mother, Jean Hermione Johnstone, was a highly respected music teacher. It was therefore virtually preordained that Andrew and his brother Julian would follow in the family's musical tradition, which both of them did.

According to William Webber, Andrew was a difficult, hyperactive child who could only be pacified with music. Though he was given a violin for his third birthday, it soon became clear that he lacked the physical dexterity that marked his younger brother Julian, who would go on to become a virtuoso cellist. Nevertheless, music was being played in the house all day long – by William Webber, by his wife, by Julian – and Andrew learned to play a variety of musical instruments, though not with exceptional skill.

He was, however, skilled at composing. In fact, he wrote his first original composition at the age of seven. He had his first piece of music published in the magazine *Music Teacher* when he was still only nine. At ten, when an aunt started taking him to see all the hit musicals, both on stage and in the cinema, he was so enthralled that he built his own, fully functioning toy theatre and gave 'performances' of his own plays, using toy soldiers, and with brother Julian playing musical accompaniment on the piano.

By this time, to supplement the classical musical education he was receiving at home, he was buying the records of Bill Haley and the Comets, Elvis Presley, Jerry Lee Lewis, Chuck Berry, Buddy Holly, Bobby Vee and the Everley Brothers. His musical tastes were becoming ever more eclectic.

'The first two records I ever heard were the *Nutcracker* suite and Elvis Presley's "Jailhouse Rock", which is a pretty fair illustration of what influenced me.'

At fourteen years of age he wrote the music (with lyrics by an older boy, Robin St Clare Barrow) for the Westminster public school pantomime, *Cinderella up the Beanstalk and Most Everywhere Else!*. During the same year he sent an idea and some songs for a musical to the Noel Gay theatrical agency, and they were impressed enough to sign him up to a short-lived contract. He also sent a demo tape to Decca Records and they sent it on to the record producer Charles Blackwell, a client to the music publisher Desmond Elliot, who also was impressed enough to sign him up. In 1963, at the age of fifteen, Lloyd Webber wrote and recorded the song 'Make Believe Love' for Charles Blackwell. Though the record was never released, young Lloyd Webber was on his way. During the same year he wrote the musical for another Westminster pantomime, *Utter Chaos or No Jeans for Venus*. A third and final show for Westminster, *Play the Fool*, was produced in June 1964.

In December, Lloyd Webber won an open exhibition to read history at Magdalen College, Oxford. However, before he went up to university, he received a letter, dated 21 April 1965, from an ambitious young songwriter, Tim Rice.

Born in 1944 in Amersham, Buckinghamshire, Rice was educated at Lancing, spent six months at the Sorbonne in Paris, worked as an articled clerk at the solicitors Pettit & Westlake, endured a brief stint as a petrol-pump attendant on a garage forecourt, attempted unsuccessfully to be a pop singer, and finally decided to become a songwriter instead. Like Lloyd Webber, he was strongly influenced not only by the rock and roll stars of the 1950s, but also by early sixties British pop: the Beatles, the Rolling Stones, the Kinks, et al. Though not a composer, Rice was a natural lyricist. One of his first songs, 'That's My Story', was released as a single by the pop group Night Shift and in May 1966, when Rice was 22, he moved to EMI to work for the bandleader and record producer Norrie Paramour. However, long before that move, Rice learned from Desmond Elliot that a talented young composer, Andrew Lloyd Webber, four years younger than Rice, was looking for a 'with-it' writer of lyrics for his songs. Impressed, Rice decided to write to Webber, asking if the two of them could meet and perhaps work together.

They did, and the rest is musical history.

The two public schoolboys, one (Lloyd Webber)

shy, the other (Rice) extrovert, but both literate and eclectic in their musical tastes, loving English classical music as well as rock and pop, soon produced their first musical, *The Likes of Us*. Based on the life of Dr Thomas Bernardo, with a book (the spoken dialogue and story-line) by the bestselling novelist Leslie Thomas, *The Likes of Us* was considered too expensive to produce and never got off the ground.

Disappointed, Webber and Rice decided to write some pop songs. On 23 June 1967 'Down Thru Summer', doubled with 'I'll Give All My Love to Southend' and sung by an attractive blonde vocalist, Ross Hannaman, became their first joint composition to be released. Alas, it went nowhere. A second single, '1969', coupled with 'Probably on Thursday', released on 27 October and also sung by Ross Hannaman, likewise failed to do much. Webber and Rice then wrote another song, 'Kansas Morning', but, before they could do anything with it, Ross Hannaman retired from the business to get married and they found no one else willing to record for them.

Towards the end of 1967, when Lloyd Webber and Rice were feeling blue, the former received a call from Alan Doggett, head of music at Colet Court, a preparatory school for St Paul's. Having taught Julian Lloyd Webber at Westminster and being an old friend of the family, Doggett knew that Andrew was a talented young composer and he wanted him to create something 'morally uplifting' for an end-of-term concert.

Excited, Lloyd Webber and Rice went to the Bible for something 'morally uplifting' and found the story of Joseph and his coat of many colours. Two months later, after working in the evenings and at weekends, with Lloyd Webber first composing the melodies and

Rice then writing the lyrics to fit, they turned out a fifteen-minute rock and roll version of the biblical story. Described as a 'pop cantata', *Joseph and his Amazing Technicolor Dreamcoat* was premiered on 1 March 1968 in Colet Court School, Hammersmith, London, to no more than polite enthusiasm from the audience of several hundred middle-class parents. However, Andrew's father, William Lloyd Webber, was so impressed by the work that he arranged for a second performance, with the work expanded to twenty minutes and performed by a rock group and full orchestra. This was performed on 12 May 1968, for an audience of 2,500, at the Central Hall, Westminster.

The jazz critic Derek Jewell, who would, from this point on, become a staunch supporter of the talented twosome, was one of those in the audience. Reviewing the piece for the *Sunday Times*, he praised the 'wonderfully singable tunes' of 'this new pop oratorio'. More importantly, he stated that this new work by 'two men in their early twenties' had proved that the pop idiom was 'capable of being used in extended form'.

Joseph and his Amazing Technicolor Dreamcoat was, in fact, the first 'pop' musical, heavily influenced by its times, and it went on in a full-length version, with over twenty songs, to be remarkably successful worldwide, playing largely to pubescent and adolescent audiences, frequently in schools and universities. This was the time of *Sergeant Pepper*, the Rolling Stones, 'electric' Dylan, love and peace, the pill and pot, Carnaby Street and the miniskirt; and it was also a time when youthful rebellion and the need to shock was at its most potent. Though heavily influenced by the attitudes and music of its period, *Joseph and the Amazing Technicolor Dreamcoat* was an innocent, simple-minded romp compared with what was coming. The notorious 'tribal love-rock' musical, *Hair*, with its nudity and barrage of four-letter words, would have its London premier on 27 September 1968, the day after the Lord Chamberlain abolished stage censorship; and though Lloyd Webber and Rice had focused on the 'love and peace' aspects of the rock revolution, rather than on sex, drugs and obscenity, they would ignore neither the success that their own pop adaptation of a biblical theme had produced nor the fact that rock and roll, as *Joseph* and *Hair* had both proven, could be used in 'extended form', blended with other musical idioms, to revitalise an exhausted genre. Such thoughts were surely foremost in their minds when they created their next work.

Jesus Christ Superstar was conceived, created and produced at a time when many leading members of the church were desperately trying to 'modernise' Christianity in the hope of attracting young converts. One of these was the Very Reverend Martin Sullivan, Dean of St Paul's Cathedral, who, impressed by the 'popularity and power' of *Joseph*, offered Webber and Rice Sir Christopher Wren's great cathedral for their next work and urged them to 'take Christ down from the stained-glass window'. After thinking it over and deciding that the events surrounding Christ and the crucifixion were 'a terrifically good story', Webber and Rice produced a full-length stage musical deliberately intended to be 'different' in that it would not, like most musicals, scatter the songs throughout the script but would, instead, have a continuous score with every word *sung*. In 1969, with the work completed, they struggled to find a title, rejecting *Jesus!*, considering *Jesus Christ* (without the exclamation mark) and finally (doubtless bearing in mind the all-important youth market with its enthusiasm for outrage) adding the word 'Superstar'. So *Jesus Christ Superstar* it came to be. Released first as a double-album in October 1970, it went on to sell two million copies in twelve months and finally made its Broadway première as a stage musical in the Mark Hellinger Theatre on 12 October the following year. It then opened in the Palace Theatre, London, on 9 August 1972.

Being a garish pop-music version of the life and crucifixion of Christ, *Jesus Christ Superstar* (1970), with its deliberately contentious title, simplified, sometimes comic story-line, religious sentiments, thunderous rock music, melodious pop songs and one showstopping ballad, stirred up the anticipated controversy ('anticipated' in the sense that this was almost certainly the intention of the young, supremely media-conscious composer and lyricist), and it became a monster success all over the world as well as a blockbuster Hollywood movie. The problem then being for the dynamic young duo: what do you do after you've done Jesus Christ?

One has to admire their chutzpah. The success of *Jesus Christ Superstar* had depended as much on the controversy it stirred up – condemnation from the church, derision from elder critics and, consequently, the support of the young – as it had on its musical score. However, for their follow-up work, Lloyd Webber suggested a musical based on P.G. Wodehouse's immensely popular books about the chinless wonder Bertie Wooster and his long-suffering butler, Jeeves, but Rice felt, correctly, that it would not work and dropped out of the project. Undaunted, Lloyd Webber went ahead with it, using the playwright Alan Ayckbourn as his new lyricist, and produced the musical *Jeeves*, which, being so far removed from the rock and pop culture – and, even worse, completely devoid of controversy – became his first and only commercial failure. Premièring at Her Majesty's Theatre, London, on 22 April 1975, it closed on 24 May, after crippling reviews and only thirty-eight performances.

A chastened Lloyd Webber hastily teamed up again with Tim Rice. Clearly aware that they needed something as controversial as *Jesus Christ Superstar* – something guaranteed to raise the interest of the critics while outraging, if not the church this time, then some high-profile organisations or individuals. Even for a relatively young, media-conscious team like Lloyd Webber and Rice, something as blatant as, say, *Hitler – The Musical* would have been a bit *too* extreme, so the life of Eva Perón, which initially seemed like an odd choice even for them, may have been chosen as a safe compromise. Certainly Eva Perón was then obscure enough, at least in the West, to render her 'safe' as a subject while being, at the same time, colourful enough to become a strong, glamorous and – infinitely more important – *controversial* lead character in a musical.

Evita Perón's life was, in fact, the personification of that old cliché of popular romantic fiction: the tale of the impoverished young country girl who flees to the big city to become a movie star, fights her way to the top through a succession of men, marries a glamorous, powerful man (in this case, her country's President), only to die, tragically, at thirty-three – the same age as Christ when he died. In other words, the Evita Perón story offered that classic, irresistible storyline – the rags-to-riches tale – with the bonus of a show-business background (Evita acted on stage, in the movies and on the radio: perfect for glamorisation) and, more crucially, particularly with regard to the PR ambitions of Lloyd Webber and Rice, a fascistic political career that would, even when simplified to fit the requirements of a musical, be certain to stir up another hornet's nest of controversy based on questions of 'good taste' and 'morality'.

Which is exactly what happened.

Premièred at the Prince Edward Theatre, London, on 21 June 1978, *Evita*, a musical in two acts, caused a sensation and no end of controversy. Lloyd Webber and Rice had already gained a great deal of publicity for the musical by releasing a double album of the score (*Evita: An Opera Based on the Life Story of Eva Perón, 1919–1952*), recorded much earlier (April–September 1976) at Olympic Studio, Barnes, London, with Julie Covington as Evita, Paul Jones as Juan Perón, C.T. Wilkinson as Ché, Tony Christie as Magaldi, and Barbara Dickson as Perón's mistress. None of these performers made it as far as the stage musical, but the album, utilising a variety of rock musicians as well as the London Philharmonic Orchestra, produced a No. 1 UK hit single in 'Don't Cry For Me Argentina'. A second song, 'Another Suitcase in Another Hall', sung by Barbara Dickson, reached No. 18 in the UK charts and the album in general received a great deal of critical attention, most of it good ('An extraordinary achievement!' – *Daily*

Mail; 'Magnificent!' – *Sunday Times*). As a device for encouraging massive media interest in the forthcoming stage musical, it certainly worked. The stage production opened not only to the usual razzmatazz of big cars, celebrities and a heavy press contingent, but, in this case, to a crowd waving banners and protesting at the use of a fascist like Eva Perón as a musical heroine.

While Tim Rice and Andrew Lloyd Webber would have been aware of the beneficial publicity to be gained from such demonstrations and, indeed, probably relished them, they were also careful to defend themselves against more serious accusations of exploitation. In this regard it can have been no accident that the notes on the studio album booklet state: '[*Evita*] is a story of people whose lives were in politics, but it is not a political story. It is a Cinderella story . . .' In fact, while the politics were skimmed over in the stage production, the more sordid aspects of the Perón/Evita regime were at least hinted at. Overall, however, the more noble aspects of Evita were emphasised. A resumé of the musical's structure is therefore worth looking at.

ACT 1 opens in 'A Cinema in Buenos Aires, July 26, 1952' when the B-film grinds to a halt and an announcement over the sound system informs the watching public that Eva Perón, spiritual leader of the nation, has died. The audience leaves in silence.

As crowds gather for the 'Requiem for Evita', we are introduced to Ché: the narrator who represents all the feelings held against Eva Perón as politician and woman. Ché mocks the funeral procession ('O What a Circus!'), sneers at Eva's reputation as a saint, and reminds us that she was merely an actress who promised all and delivered nothing to her people. Then he leads us back to the beginning of her life.

Eva Duarte is fifteen years old and living in a desolate small Argentine town when she meets a professional nightclub singer, Agustin Magaldi, performing 'On This Night of a Thousand Stars'. After becoming involved with him ('Eva and Magaldi') she begs him to take her to Buenos Aires and he tries putting her off with 'Eva, Beware of the City'. Undaunted, she leaves town with him and arrives excitedly in the city of her dreams, summed up in the exuberant 'Buenos Aires'.

Having used Magaldi and finding no further use for him, Eva ruthlessly drops him ('Goodnight and Thank You') and goes on to become a minor actress ('The Lady's Got Potential') mainly on radio. At a 'Charity Concert' she meets the politically powerful Juan Perón, instantly charms him ('I'd Be Surprisingly Good for You') and leaves the concert with him.

Moving into Perón's residence, Eva turfs out his mistress ('Another Suitcase in Another Hall'), installs herself in the girl's place and soon becomes Perón's strongest ally, even though she is roundly despised by the military and the Oligarchy (the ruling classes) who view her as a whore and describe her as 'Dangerous Jade.' Nevertheless, Evita pushes Perón into using the support of the common people to have himself voted in as President and create 'A New Argentina'.

ACT 2 begins in 1946 with the announcement 'On the Balcony of the Casa Rosada' that Juan Perón has been elected President. Eva then addresses the people, reminding them that she and Perón are their choice and, as such, represent the heart and soul of the people ('Don't Cry For Me Argentina').

Married to Perón and revered as a saint by the people ('High Flying, Adored'), Eva, now known as Evita, decides to become a roaming ambassador for Argentina ('Rainbow High') and sets off on her soon-to-be-notorious 'Rainbow Tour'. She receives a rapturous welcome in Spain, but is either insulted or snubbed everywhere else and returns home, humiliated, but determined to take revenge on the ruling classes of her own country ('The Actress Hasn't Learned the Lines You'd Like to Hear'). Crushing the Oligarchy's other charity organisations, she forms her own charity, the Eva Perón Foundation, which both makes and loses money at a prodigious rate ('And The Money Keeps Rolling In [And Out]'). Nevertheless, because of her bizarre charity, Evita becomes a saint to the people ('Santa Evita'). Though refusing to acknowledge her own failings as a politician and aware that her time is running out because she is dying ('Waltz for Eva and Ché'), she continues to fight for Perón and he acknowledges that she is his greatest attribute ('She Is a Diamond') without whom he could not survive politically.

However, the political situation is on the move again ('Dice are Rolling') and Evita insists upon running for Vice-President. Perón explains that he cannot make this happen, that it would be politically dangerous, and though Evita is now desperately ill, she intends to keep fighting ('Eva's Sonnet'). Defeated in her bid for the Vice-Presidency, Evita offers 'Eva's Final Broadcast' and then, in her final hours, relives her life ('Don't Cry For Me Argentina'/'Montage'). With her final words, 'Lament', she expresses no regrets and begs the people to understand what she has done and remember her always. In an attempt to ensure that this happens, Perón's 'Embalmers' move in to preserve her dead body.

A 'Cinderella' story, indeed. While the treatment was disingenuous, romanticising a tyrant ('I know she's a bitch,' Rice had said to Lloyd Webber, 'but let's make her a wonderful bitch'), it failed to thrill the more politicised critics. Harold Prince's direction and the spectacular lighting effects of David Hersey came in for almost unanimous praise; the vocal skills of Elaine Page (Evita) and the acting talents of Joss Ackland (Juan Perón), David Essex (Ché) and Mark Ryan (Magaldi) received the usual mixed reviews (though by and large they all came off with flying colours and Page, in particular, became an overnight star); and the Andrew Lloyd Webber score and Tim Rice lyrics were generally well received. The critics were, however, sharply divided on other aspects of the work and were particularly incensed by its political naïveté or, as some had it, its disingenuousness. Let us quote from a few of them.

'In its deployment of light, space and bodies,' said Robert Cushman (*Observer* 25 June 1978), '*Evita* sets new standards for the West End . . .' Cushman went on to praise the director Harold 'Hal' Prince, choreographer Larry Fuller, lighting effects specialist David Hersey, and the show's designers Timothy O'Brien and Tazeena Firth, for 'a sustained feat of imaginative animation'. However, he qualified this high praise by stating that the show was finally 'unsatisfactory' because it took 'no obvious party line' and told us little about its central characters.

While Tim Rice's lyrics were 'reasonably intelligent' and Andrew Lloyd Webber's music 'more than reasonably melodious', neither had illuminated the subject matter or helped to produce characters we could truly care about.

Michael Billington (*Guardian*, 22 June 1978) deemed the show 'an audacious and fascinating musical' that was staged with 'breathtaking inventiveness and quicksilver fluency'. In his view, the staging of Hal Prince was 'a miracle which every British musical director ought to go and study'. However, although he also praised the 'beautiful score' of Andrew Lloyd Webber ('full of a strange, inviolate sadness') he, too, was miffed that Lloyd Webber and Rice had adopted a tone of 'fence-sitting neutrality towards their protagonists' and that, 'hooked on style, they seem unconcerned with substance'. Like Cushman, he complained about their avoidance of the more repellent realities of the Perón reign; though he concluded that *Evita* was, in the end, 'an experience that compensates for many wasted nights spent watching British musicals.'

Financial Times reviewer Michael Coveney declared the show to be a 'stunningly well-organised and beautiful production' and added that 'in terms of presentation, the show is breathtaking'. However, in line with his fellow critics, he then went on to say that, 'In terms of content, it is irredeemably paltry . . . a banal confection overblown in a trumpet of sound and movement . . .' The show was hampered by 'lusciously orchestrated pop melody to decorate quite ordinary lyrics' and the 'real star of the evening' was its director, Hal Prince.

This line of thought continued with Milton

Shulman in the *Evening Standard*, who was 'captivated and intrigued by the melodic flow of [Lloyd] Webber's music, the sharp, brittle lyrics by Tim Rice, the confident skill of Harold Prince's direction and the overall impression that here at last is a British musical that is as mature, adventurous and technically adroit as anything the Americans have sent us in recent years.' (Shulman fails to mention that Harold Prince is an *American* director – a fact that may have accounted for the widely praised visual brilliance of the London production.) However, like his fellow critics, Shulman was incensed that the brutal politics of the Peróns' regime had been 'reduced to kindergarten history' and that the book presented a 'generally threadbare synopsis of historical events'. Also like other critics, he was not amused by the fact that Tim Rice had introduced a 'shadowy commentator vaguely modelled on Ché Guevara' even though (as Michael Coveney had also pointed out) Ché Guevara, apart from being of Argentine origin, had no place in the actual story of Eva Perón.

Perhaps the most politically damning of all was John Peter's *Sunday Times* review which opened with: '*Evita* is a superb musical, but its heart is rotten. It is a glittering homage to a monster.' He goes on to describe it as 'a glamorous, sentimental fairy tale about a murderous Cinderella'. While acknowledging that Lloyd Webber and Rice had produced a show that 'throbs and pulsates with the demonic energy of its heroine' and describing it as 'one of the very best stage musicals London has seen in years', Peter does at least take the trouble to remind his readers that the real Evita was an unscrupulous fascist who ruled not only by glamour, but by coercion, repression and torture. Bearing this in mind, Peter was forced to conclude that *Evita* 'joins the long line of British musicals which have nothing to do with their own time. You're left with the spectacle . . .'

How could Hollywood not be interested? Here was a potential movie musical with glamour, romance, sex and violence, based on a stage musical widely praised for its 'spectacular' production values and accused of having no genuine, or contentious, political analysis. It was, in other words, a potentially 'hot' movie musical about a controversial subject that had, thank God, been shorn of any material that could seriously be a threat to Hollywood's worldwide markets. Even better, it had been directed by a famed *American* director and was being sold on its spectacle and glamour. It just had to have legs.

Certainly it had legs in the theatre. On 25 September 1979, approximately fifteen months after it had opened in London and while the London production was still packing them in, *Evita* premièred at the Broadway Theatre, New York, starring Patti Lu Pone, Mandy Patinkin, Bob Gunson, Mark Syers and Jane Ohringer. On 20 January 1981, it opened at the Theater an der Wien, Vienna, and on 10 September 1982, it had its German première at the Theater des Westens, Berlin. Over the years there were more productions in Australia, New Zealand, Japan, Hungary, Spain, Austria, Mexico, South Africa and Brazil, with all of them accompanied by the release of their original cast-recording albums. The London production won two Olivier Awards (Best Musical and Best Performance); the New York production won seven Tony awards (Best Musical, Best Actress, Best Score, Best Featured Actor, Best Lighting, Best Book, Best

Director); and the original studio album produced a third hit single, 'Oh What A Circus!' (David Essex) which reached No. 3 in the UK charts. All in all, *Evita* made a fortune and continues to do so, with new productions opening every year all over the world.

So *naturally* Hollywood was interested.

The role of Evita soon became the most sought-after since *Gone with the Wind*'s Scarlett O'Hara. For years, as the stage musical continued to meet with stunning success worldwide, rumours flew thick and fast regarding who would be directing the film version and who would play the lead. When, in 1995, after many false starts and stops, it was announced that Alan Parker would be directing and Madonna starring as Evita, the latter choice was greeted with widespread condemnation and derision. Nevertheless, few major female stars could be more suitable for the role and few wanted it, or needed it, quite as badly as did Madonna. This is because there are striking similarities between her and Evita.

Most of what we have seen in Evita we can also see in Madonna when we examine her life and motivation. There are, of course, differences, but the similarities are greater. Indeed, in its own distinctive, modern way, Madonna's life is a replay of the life of Evita Perón: a rags-to-riches tale in which early personal loss is a motivating factor and in which, once success is achieved, ruthless will is deployed to sustain it. So let us look at Madonna before she is reincarnated as 'Saint' Evita. We will see where she comes from.

Chapter Twenty-One

Like Evita, Madonna came from a working-class background and, if not initially poor, was compelled to watch her family sliding into bad times. Her father, Silvio Ciccone, the youngest son of a large Italian-American family, was born and raised in Pittsburgh, gained a degree in engineering, worked for various car companies in the Detroit area (then known as Motor Town, soon to be famous as Motown) and eventually ended up working for General Dynamics. In 1955 he married a French-Canadian, Madonna Fortin, of Bay City, on Lake Huron's Saginaw Bay, and the pair settled down in Rochester, Detroit, to have a family. They had two sons, Anthony and Martin, then, on 16 August 1959, seven years after the death of Evita Perón, their first daughter Louise Veronica, was born.

Three more children followed – a sister, Paula, another brother, Christopher, and a second sister, Melanie – six children in all. The family struggled to survive against difficult odds and then, when she was only thirty years old, Madonna Fortin Ciccone died of breast cancer.

Years later, when the first daughter, Louise Veronica, had taken on her mother's name, Madonna, and become rich and famous, she would insist that she never fully recovered from her mother's early death, which occurred when she, Louise Veronica (Madonna), was only six years old.

164

Indeed, she would later feel empathy for Evita Perón because she, too, had lost a parent, her father, at an early age – in her case when she was only seven years old. Even worse was the fact that Madonna's father remarried a few years later when Madonna was still grieving for her mother; a situation similar to that of Evita Perón when, shortly after the death of her father, her mother became the *casa chica*, or mistress, of a male 'protector'.

'I remember it being really hard for me,' Madonna has said, 'to get the word "mother" out of my mouth. It was really painful.'

Feeling abandoned by her mother and betrayed by her father, Madonna would never really learn to live comfortably with herself and developed a variety of neuroses, including fear of cancer, the fear of losing her father, and, as part of a deeply religious Catholic family, fear of the Devil. These fears made her desperate for attention and she went all out to get it.

During the slow, agonising death of their mother, as she had gradually weakened and lost control, the kids had turned wild, forcing Madonna, in this family of six children, to fight for attention and for her rights. Eventually, however, with his wife gone, Silvio Ciccone brought in a succession of housekeepers to keep the children in order. This distanced him from the children and made Madonna, in particular, yearn even more for attention.

In all fairness, Silvio Ciccone was also distanced from his children because he was compelled to work long hours to sustain them. He was also a stern man, an Italian-American Catholic who, like his immigrant parents, deeply believed in Old World values: sexual modesty, discipline, hard work, religious worship.

Confused within herself, Madonna would alternately respect and reject such beliefs, eventually retaining some, such as hard work and discipline, while boldly rebelling against others, such as sexual modesty. These contradictions would indelibly stamp her character and shape her whole future.

In childhood, however, because of the loss of her mother and what she felt was a betrayal by her father when he married one of his housekeepers, she craved attention and did everything in her power to get it. From an early age she detested conformity and, at the same time, realised that one way of getting attention was to be flagrantly nonconformist, or 'different'. Already compelled to endure her father's Old World brand of Catholicism – practically no television viewing, no cinema at all, few popular magazines allowed in the house – she rebelled against the conformity of her Catholic school, the Holy Family Regional School in Rochester, by wearing brightly coloured underpants instead of regulation knickers. She also liked to display them either by raising her skirt or by hanging upside down from the monkey bars in the school playground. Blessed with dark hair, good looks and a winning smile, she danced on tables at family get-togethers, became a precocious ten-year-old flirt, and learned how to wrap her normally stern father, as well as other adults, around her little finger.

Nine months in convent school did little to dampen her spirits, though it appears to have extinguished her early desire to be a nun and replaced it with the lasting desire to be a movie star or some other kind of celebrity.

The outrageous behaviour continued. She angered her father by wearing pants to church and once even

166

attended church naked under her coat, giggling throughout the service with a friend who had come similarly attired. She stole apples and went on shoplifting sprees. While still twelve years old, in the seventh grade, she shocked the parishioners attending a St Andrew's annual talent show by prancing onto the stage covered in green fluorescent paint, wearing what looked like a skimpy bikini, and gyrating her hips as Goldie Hawn was then doing in the *Laugh In* show. At thirteen she acted in a super-8 movie short directed by one of her classmates and, for one of the scenes, allowed an egg to be 'fried' on her bare belly. For these reasons and others, by the time she was in her teens she had gained a reputation as being loud-mouthed and forward.

As Madonna takes a delight in shocking her public, her own comments about her sexual nature must be taken with a pinch of salt. She has claimed that she first kissed a boy when she was still only ten years old, after tearing off her school blazer and blouse and chasing him around the school yard. Madonna has since insisted that, from adolescence on, she was interested in all aspects of sexuality. However, her much discussed bisexuality, whether real or imagined, certainly did not appear to be prevalent at school, where, according to friends, she showed an interest only in boys. She was, however, uncommonly bold when it came to getting the boys she fancied, rarely waiting to be asked for a date and instead reversing the normal run of things by asking them out. For this reason, rather than sexual promiscuity, she was soon labelled a 'nympho' by the boys and a 'slut' by the girls. Given her need to shock and gain attention, almost certainly she would have enjoyed this reputation and, given the comments of old friends, appears to have done so.

If we are to believe her own comments, she lost her virginity at fifteen in the back of the Cadillac of one Russell Long and did so with the same pragmatic determination as she was then displaying in most activities and would later apply to her show business career. According to Long, losing her virginity to him had little to do with love, affection or lust.

'It was more to do with adventure, of the experience of the unknown. She really wanted to find out what it was like.'

Virgin or not, she continued to rebel. After fighting once too often with her father over religion, she was transferred to the Rochester West Junior High where, her father assumed, she would be more disciplined. In fact, the move merely increased her urge to be different. She stopped shaving her legs and armpits, wore hot pants or bell-bottom hip-huggers, and set her hair in a wide variety of styles. Also, she became obsessed with boys and music, though the latter seems to have been the greater passion. She listened constantly to pop records – Stevie Wonder, Frankie Lymon, Carol King – and was quick to give her opinion about them. A lot of her friends were then forming groups and she wasn't shy about joining them. Every source has indicated that she was a 'natural' from the very start, keen to perform and fearless when it came to doing so.

'She would just dance like you could not believe,' said a friend, Lori Jahns. 'She could really do it.'

The ability to 'really do it' from the beginning may have sprung from the fact that Madonna didn't care what anyone thought about her and was supremely unselfconscious when performing in public. She was, however, very conscious of how she wanted to be perceived – she still craved attention – so by the time she was, with the other girls, into necking in the movie theatres, she had become a Marilyn Monroe fan and already created her own 'floozy' look: wearing stuffed bras, tight sweaters and lots of lipstick.

By now, her fascination with pop music and the movies had fused into the single passion that was to dominate her life. When not drooling over movie and teen magazines (just as Evita had done), already imagining herself as Marilyn Monroe, complete with Marilyn's 'lost' mother and parental abandonment neuroses, she would be dancing to Motown records – mostly the all-girl groups such as Martha and the Vandellas, the Shirelles, the Ronettes and, of course, Diana Ross and the Supremes – in the houses of friends and invariably inventing her own routines.

Dance soon became her passion and she took every class she could, eventually coming under the wing of a ballet teacher, Christopher Flynn. A practising Catholic who made no secret of being gay, he broadened her cultural interests by taking her to museums and art galleries, as well as to the gay clubs and discothèques of downtown Detroit. As sex was rarely discussed in blue-collar Detroit, Madonna was enthralled at the conversation and behaviour of the gay community, soon feeling even more comfortable with them than she did with her 'straight' friends. The gay community also encouraged her natural exhibitionism and this, too, made her feel at one with them. She danced relentlessly, superbly, in the discothèques and received a lot of attention.

According to Flynn, when Madonna danced, 'She was hot.' Flynn also confirms that Madonna's hunger for new experiences was virtually 'insatiable'. She was a sponge soaking everything up and changing virtually every day.

Certainly, her hunger for attention was undiminished and she continued to get it by being outrageous. In a dance class at the University of Michigan, to which she had graduated on a scholarship in 1976, she reduced the class to howls of laughter by belching loudly during an elegant *plié* exercise. During a summer's day, she asked if she could take off her leotards and just wear a bra without knickers. Also, apart from being as outrageous as she could, she was moving from her 'floozy' look to a 'punk' image by wearing her hair short and spiky, ripping pieces out of her leotards and deliberately having runs in her tights. By now her body had matured voluptuously and she was eager to flaunt it.

Having introduced Madonna to so much that was new, exciting and, by blue-collar standards, deliciously shocking, Flynn encouraged her to fly to New York. Thus, like Evita, Madonna left home to seek, in her own words, 'fame and fortune'.

Chapter Twenty-Two

In 1978, nineteen years old, Madonna flew into New York on an $88 Northwest Airlines ticket and had no more good experiences for a long time. After spending an initial two weeks in the house of a good samaritan, she drifted from one slum to another, finally settling into an apartment at 232 East 4th Street in the notorious Lower East Side. ('The place was crawling with cockroaches. There were winos in the hallways and the entire place smelled like stale beer.') She lived mainly on popcorn and the occasional apple and, according to legend, though this may be apocryphal, dined out of the rubbish bins in the streets.

Though reportedly not free with her sexual favours, she was adroit at encouraging handouts from interested men and managed to survive long enough to pick up work. A spell as a hat-check girl in the fashionable Russian Tea Room on West 57th was followed by work with Dunkin' Donuts and then Burger King. Nude modelling followed: first for art classes, then in private homes and, eventually, for professional pin-up photographers.

Though Madonna has often claimed that she didn't mind doing this kind of work – and while some of the photographers have stated, perhaps self-servingly, that she was good at it and appeared to enjoy it – it is revealing that years later, when she was famous and the nude photos resurfaced in *Playboy*, *Penthouse* and other magazines worldwide, she was heard to complain. In other words, while she did not, like Eva Duarte, actually succumb to the 'casting couch' she certainly had experiences not dissimilar to Evita's and may, at the time, have viewed them with more distaste than she now admits to.

One such experience was her part in a soft-porn movie, *A Certain Sacrifice*, involving a rape scene, an orgiastic dance sequence and a ritual sacrifice. Madonna was paid only $100 for her appearance and often insisted that it hadn't bothered her to make it. However, many years later, when *High Society* magazine paid $100,000 for out-take nudes from the film to be sold as pictures to men's magazines, Madonna was outraged and tried to stop the pictures being used. She failed. Eventually the out-takes were published worldwide and the movie itself ended up on the porno video shelves.

Nevertheless, to the ambitious 20-year-old Madonna, these were at least ways of making the rent money and she was otherwise working hard on her show-business ambitions.

By the beginning of 1980, in the decade of 'flash trash', she was still seeking attention by hanging out in New York bars wearing minimalist clothes (hardly more than her underwear) or parading the sleazy Lower East Side of New York in outrageous outfits. She went out with graffiti artists, spraying her own name on the walls. She did everything she could to be outrageous and get herself attention – but she also kept working. Thirteen weeks of training with the famed Alvin Ailey American Dance Theater were followed by further training with Pearl Lang, a protégé of the dance legend, Martha Graham.

'She was an exceptional dancer,' Lang said.

'Madonna had the power, the intensity, to go beyond mere performance into something more exciting . . . Madonna simply has the magical quality that a great artist needs.'

Nevertheless, after an argument with Lang (and Madonna was always quick to disagree with anyone, no matter how famous), she moved out of her apartment at 232 East 4th Street and into an abandoned synagogue in Corona, Queens, which she shared with two musician brothers, Dan and Ed Gilroy. The Gilroys had a rock band, the Breakfast Club, featuring an attractive blonde, Angie Smith, who played bass and dressed in slinky, see-through dresses, or 'several strings of beads loosely sewed together'. Madonna, then still dark-haired, joined the group as a back-up vocalist and became a foil to Smith, thus learning to project her sensual self even more.

However, at the end of her first year with the group, she left to dance and sing back-up for the discothèque pin-up, Patrick Hernandez, working with him in Paris, France. Though given a voice coach and the support of two French producers, Jean Claude Pellerin and Jean Van Lieu, who had vowed to turn her into 'the new Edith Piaf', she rebelled at their disciplines, despised their French snobbery, and resented the fact that they had really brought her to Paris just to 'show their friends what they had found in the gutters of New York'. Increasingly fed up, she spent more time in the nightclubs and cafés than she did working, and eventually packed her bags and returned to New York, where she picked up again with the Breakfast Club.

This reunion with her old friends became a pivotal point in her career. Now, she was not only singing back-up and dancing with the group, but also writing songs, learning to play any instrument that the others would help her with, and also managing the group's business affairs, finding them engagements, and trying to set up record deals, using her considerable charm where and when needed – rather as Evita had done with the military junta. Eventually, however, her restless (some would say 'ruthless') ambitions made her insist that she sing solo in the band. When Gilroy refused, she left the group and moved out of the synagogue in Queens, determined to make it on her own.

'I was just a lot more goal-oriented and commercial than they were,' she later said pragmatically of Breakfast Club. 'I took advantage of the situation because I knew I could make it work to my benefit.'

Enlisting the aid of her old friend, Steve Bray, the black, pony-tailed drummer who had worked the Detroit lounge circuit with a local band while also working as a waiter in the Blue Frogge nightclub, she formed her own group. Egocentric as always, the centre of her own world, she wanted to call the group 'Madonna', but Bray talked her out of it and the group was called the Millionaires instead. When this name brought them no luck, they changed to Modern Dance, then, incongruously, to Emmy, at which point Madonna made a demo tape. Camille Barbone, a partner in Adam Alter's Gotham Management, which had its own recording studio in New York's Music City, eventually heard the tape, which included the song 'Everybody'. Liking its promise of good old-fashioned rock and roll, she fixed up a contract and allowed Madonna to rename the group 'Madonna'.

After moving to New York's Upper West Side,

Madonna threw herself passionately into the job of selling the group and, through it, herself. During the day, she wrote songs with Steve Bray – more funk than rock and roll – and they performed those songs each night at the Roxy or the Dancetaria. The latter was a four-floor Chelsea disco that specialised in funky music and attracted exotics, many in skin-tight leather and chains with purple or phosphorescent-green hair. Madonna responded to this exotica by wearing clothing torn in all the right places, exposing her belly, draping herself with glittering Maripol jewellery, and wearing her 'Boy Toy' belt, which, combined with her erotic dancing, purposefully encouraged her 'slut' image.

Like Evita, Madonna often secretly yearned to be a man – or, at least, to have the freedom that men have – and this masculine side to her nature made her even more aggressive when it came to getting what she wanted. Because this scared off many heterosexual males, she felt easier with gay men and, indeed, was 'constantly falling in love' with such. She was also, however, in the words of Camille Barbone, 'a sexual creature' who had 'men eating out of her hands'.

By this time, Madonna was openly describing herself as a 'Boy Toy' who, like Evita Perón, had a wide variety of men in areas where they could be of help to her. But Barbone insists that Madonna was not sleeping with any of them and that her unique ability was to get them to help her, with loans of money or unpaid musical skills, without actually putting out for them – another skill she shared with Evita. Madonna only had affairs when she was genuinely attracted to the man involved. She did not turn sexual tricks for favours – she used only her charm.

Nevertheless, around the New York clubs she had developed the reputation of being a 'prick-teaser' because she liked to be looked at and dressed to ensure that men stared at her. According to various reports, she was sexy, flirtatious, outspoken, fascinating and frightening in equal measures. This made her attractive to men who were in a position to help her – and a great many did.

By 1981, though Madonna had made a four-cut tape at the Gotham Studio in New York's Music Building and had developed a cult following in the New Wave clubs, her relationship with Gotham Management was breaking down due to differences in opinion about what direction her career should be taking. Gotham Management wanted Madonna to continue playing raucous rock and roll, but Madonna wanted to go the disco route and, also, to include some of the ballads she had recently started writing. Also, though Gotham had produced Madonna's first four cuts and publicised her at great expense, so far they hadn't managed to sell the tapes and their money was running out.

By early 1982, because of their various conflicts and problems, both creative and financial, the relationship between Gotham and Madonna had degenerated beyond the point of repair. Determined to break away, Madonna deliberately flirted with the young record-producer and disc jockey Mark Kamins, then a firm favourite on the New Wave club scene and performing regularly at the Dancetaria. She and Kamins soon started doing the clubs together and eventually, confident that Kamins was seriously interested in her, Madonna gave him a four-cut demo that she had made with Steve Bray on an ordinary tape recorder. Kamins loved the tape and played it every night to an ecstatic crowd in the Dancetaria. Excited by the response, he contacted Michael Rosenblatt, a rising young executive at Sire Records, the New Wave arm of the huge Warner Brothers Communication Group. Aware that Rosenblatt was a 'dance-mix' master producer and that Madonna was a dance-orientated act, Kamins begged him to listen to the tape. When Rosenblatt did so, he was instantly smitten and agreed to sign 'this incredibly attractive female singer' to Warner Brothers' Sire Records.

Madonna's day had arrived.

Chapter Twenty-Three

Madonna soon proved just how ruthless she could be when it came to her career. Though the Sire contract was for Madonna alone, Bray was happy because he would be producing the first single. Similarly, Kamins thought he would be repaid for his efforts by producing Madonna's first album. Madonna, however, had other ideas.

Aware that the wrong kind of production could ruin this golden opportunity, she decided that Bray and Kamins would have to be dropped and someone more experienced put in charge. In the event, the head of Sire Records, Seymour Stein, though impressed with Madonna, decided initially to commit only to three twelve-inch singles against a modest advance of $5,000, with the possibility of an album later, depending upon the fate of the singles. The question of using, or not using, Kamins could therefore be delayed, though her good friend, Steve Bray, had to be dropped.

'I just didn't trust him enough,' Madonna said.

Consequently, during Easter 1982, Madonna went into the studio for a remake of 'Everybody', coupled with 'Ain't No Big Deal', produced by Mark Kamins.

Putting together a stage act to publicise the single, she bleached her hair blonde and hired three dancers, including the gay artist Martin Burgoyne, with whom she had previously roomed. Lip-synching to the single when it was aired at the Dancetaria, Madonna and her three dancers, Erica, Bags and Burgoyne, gave a sensational, erotically charged performance. As the single was also being played on the airwaves, they gave the same performance in as wide a variety of clubs as possible – New Wave, disco, hard rock, gay, black, transvestite – to push the single into the top ten of the dance charts and encourage Sire Records to bankroll the first album.

Before the album was produced, however, the video wizard Ed Steinberg was commissioned to produce a video for the 'Everybody' single. Thrilled to find that Madonna could 'sing, dance and act incredibly well', Steinberg put together a video that emphasised her unique, streetwise dancing and erotic appeal. As a result of the sensational video, 'Everybody' shot up to No. 3 on the dance charts, cracked the top 100 pop hits, and reached sales of over 250,000.

Now it was Mark Kamins' turn to be dropped.

Realising that she was on the brink of success and concerned, correctly, that a single mistake could wreck her golden opportunity, Madonna decided that she needed a producer more experienced than Kamins. As a consequence, Kamins was ruthlessly axed and the second twelve-inch single, 'Physical Attraction', and first album, *Madonna*, were produced by Reggie 'Roberta Flack' Lucas.

While the single became another hit in the dance charts, it did not crack the pop charts and the album, released in July 1983, was likewise not an instant success. 'Holiday', the first single from the album, though released with great hopes, also reached the top of the dance charts but failed to make a dent in the pop charts, but 'Burning Up', accompanied by a stunningly sexy video, broke through and also made her an icon of the MTV generation. When, in 1984, she followed 'Burning Up' with 'Borderline' and 'Lucky Star', both singles – both also done as sexually charged videos – she became a chart-topper at last. 'Lucky Star' pushed the *Madonna* album over the one-million mark and Madonna was on her way.

Nevertheless, convinced that the relative lack of chart success of her first album was due to Reggie Lucas's pop orientated production when she really wanted disco, she had Lucas dropped – just as she had dropped Bray and Kamins – and asked for Nile Rodgers, producer of David Bowie and Duran Duran, to mastermind her next album, eventually entitled *Like A Virgin*. Not content with this, she went to Freddy Demann, manager of Michael Jackson and reportedly the best in the business, and asked him to take over her management. After watching her perform at New York's trendy Studio 54, Demann agreed to do so.

Given Demann's business acumen, Rodgers' brilliant production talents, and a good selection of songs, four co-written by Madonna and Steve Bray, the *Like A Virgin* album could hardly lose. But what really made it take off and marked Madonna's future course indelibly – a career based on calculated controversy – was the video for the first single release, which was the album's title track.

Shot in Venice, Italy, in July 1984, the video for the 'Like A Virgin' single was a carefully calculated piece of erotica that utilised the Venice locations in a dreamlike manner while creating two distinct images of its star: the innocent young girl in a flowing white, virginal dress – a lamb lying with the lion – and the bare-bellied, streetwise tart, gyrating sensually and pressing her belly to phallic columns as she sang, 'You make me feel . . . like a virgin'. The result was an avalanche of condemnation from elderly media pundits and the morally 'correct' – words such as 'prostitution', 'tramp', 'slut', 'porn queen' and 'trashy tart' were dispensed liberally between the customary psychosexual pop theorising – and, more helpfully, a massive wave of approval from the largely pubescent MTV generation, who loved Madonna all the more for being offensive.

The analogy here is not with Marilyn Monroe, whom Madonna continued to revere, but with Elvis Presley during the 1950s. Elvis's stage performances were also viewed by the elder generation as obscene and brought an avalanche of condemnation upon him – but, the more he was condemned by the establishment, the more the teenagers loved him. So it was with Madonna and her videos. The more she was pilloried from the pulpit and by the media, the more the kids loved her. She became a teen heroine.

Small wonder that she continued with her outrageous videos, each more blatantly provocative than the last and edging inexorably towards a deliberately provocative mingling of religion and sex – the bared belly and the crucifix; the thrusting crotch and the altar – which many viewed, and condemned, as blasphemous. Even *Rolling Stone* magazine, which had long extolled the virtues of rock music's essential outrageousness, was moved to complain about Madonna's 'bare-bellied, fondle-my-bra image' and 'sex sells routine'. But sales of lacy lingerie, all-over lace body briefers, black push-up bras – and, yes, crucifixes to be worn as mere adornments – to teenage girls soared as the Madonna bandwagon raced on.

181

Released in December 1984, the *Like A Virgin* album soon reached No. 1 on the *Billboard* charts, the single simultaneously reached No. 1 on the singles chart, and the subsequent Virgin Tour, during which Madonna's stage performances were as provocative as her videos, played to nearly 400,000 fans in twenty-seven cities.

Though the combined appeal of her outrageous videos, quasi-pornographic stage performances and sluttish media image soon had Hollywood knocking on Madonna's door, she actually made her first 'real' movie just before the album and tour made her a megastar. Though she had already appeared in the soft-porn video, *A Certain Sacrifice*, and had also played a cameo role as a nightclub chanteuse, singing two of her own songs, in the instantly forgotten *Visionquest* (entitled *Crazy For You* in the United Kingdom), her first real movie was Susan Seidelman's *Desperately Seeking Susan*.

Seidelman's first, small-budget, movie, *Smithereens*, had been a surprise hit at the 1982 Cannes Film Festival and gained her a reputation as a quirky, idiosyncratic talent. For her second movie, which would also have a small budget, she chose *Desperately Seeking Susan*, a quirky, idiosyncratic comedy about a bored New Jersey housewife, Roberta (Rosanna Arquette), who dreams of living a more exciting life and becomes intrigued by a love affair being conducted through the personal ads, where a nameless young man is 'desperately seeking' a girl called Susan (Madonna). Through one of the oldest plot devices in cinema – insomnia – Roberta comes to live Susan's life and is changed dramatically by the experience.

Though Arquette, a cultish actress of formidable

talent, is the nominal star of the film, she fades help-
lessly into the background whenever Madonna is on
screen. Whether or not what Madonna does in this
movie can be called acting, her personification of a
sluttish, manipulating, fiercely independent kook is
every bit as mesmerising as Brigitte Bardot's insou-
ciant sexuality in *And God Created Woman*. In fact,
whether 'acting' or simply being herself (the compar-
ison with Bardot is apt), Madonna becomes the 'star'
of *Desperately Seeking Susan* and creates, perhaps by
recreating herself, an indelible character.

The critics, by and large, praised the performance,
though many, in referring to her 'sluttishness', albeit
'delightful' (*Newsweek*), were assuming that the
Susan portrayed on screen was no more than a thinly
disguised portrayal of the real Madonna.

Hurtling towards an artistic cul-de-sac, Madonna
continued exploiting her sluttish image while combining it with her growing obsession with cinema
and, perhaps inevitably, with Marilyn Monroe. Her
work on *Desperately Seeking Susan* had begun in
November 1984 when the *Like A Virgin* album was
released. By the end of that year both the album and
the single were at the top of the charts and the
'Material Girl' single was equally successful. For the
video of the latter, shot early in 1985, Madonna
finally gave in fully to her Marilyn Monroe obsession
by blatantly imitating her – a ruby-lipped platinum-
blonde, wearing virtually the same skin-tight, shock-
ing-pink, split-to-the-thigh dress that Marilyn had
worn in *Gentlemen Prefer Blondes*.

The obsession with Monroe was more than an
artistic device, or an excuse to let Madonna change
her image. Indeed, shortly after the 'Material Girl'

video was produced, Madonna, then deeply involved with the eccentric, often violent actor Sean Penn, had him drive her to Monroe's grave in Westwood Cemetery, Los Angeles. Reportedly, Madonna was visibly shaking when she reached the grave and found a fresh rose, placed there by Marilyn's former husband, the legendary baseball player Joe DiMaggio.

From this point on, Madonna's identification with Monroe would deepen alarmingly. In 1986 she posed as a Monroe lookalike for *Life* magazine; in 1991 she was doing the same for the Italian *Vogue* and the international *Vanity Fair*; and a few weeks later she appeared as a Monroe identikit, wearing a short, black dress, at a Beverley Hills Benefit concert. The 'Material Girl' and 'Papa Don't Preach' videos both lean heavily on the Monroe image, and her performance as the *femme fatale*, Breathless Mahoney, in Warren Beatty's *Dick Tracy*, was virtually a Monroe impersonation.

This fixation stems from Madonna's identification with Monroe's great childhood loss (her mother was committed to an asylum shortly after she was born, she never knew who her father was, and she spent most of her childhood years in orphanages) and with her subsequent battle, against all the odds, to break away from that childhood and become one of the most famous women of her time. Madonna wanted the very same: to escape from the fears engendered by the early death of her mother and become the greatest star in the firmament. In this sense, Marilyn Monroe was her role model.

Madonna's identification with Evita Perón has similar roots and has made her feel that the role is perfect for her. The parallels are intriguing. Like Madonna,

Evita began as an impoverished brunette and then became a platinum-blonde performer. Like Madonna, Evita lost a parent when still a child. Like Madonna's mother, Evita died early from cancer. Like Madonna, Evita was obliged to use men to get what she wanted. Also, Madonna had taken her mother's name for its religious connotations (such a name could only make her shock tactics all the more blasphemous) and Evita, in the end, had been called the 'madonna' by her people. Finally, in 1976 Evita, the 'madonna', became the unlikely subject of a rock opera and Madonna was, of course, a rock singer.

Though these comparisons are striking, they are not the only reasons why Madonna would identify with Evita. Indeed, Madonna's one-time husband, the troubled actor Sean Penn, was widely viewed as a rebel and Madonna admired rebellious figures; but she particularly admired *women* who had suffered loss in early life and yet managed to fight their way to success against all the odds. In this respect, she would have seen Evita as a role model – even more so than Marilyn.

Though Madonna had always loved Marilyn and was respectful of her courage, she had also insisted publicly that Marilyn had been a *victim*, which she, Madonna, was not. Evita Perón, on the other hand, though also emerging from a blighted childhood, had never let herself be a victim and had, instead, used her deprivations as a motivating force. Madonna, who could not resist dramatising her own childhood loss and fears, but who had, at least, used them as spring-boards to personal freedom, would have identified strongly with Evita's courage and ruthless ambition. Evita's politics had nothing to do with it: it was her *soul* – its odd mixture of the male and the female, its hunger for success and power – with which Madonna identified.

'Only *I* can do Eva Perón,' she once said. 'She went hungry like me, and like me she left her home town in order to succeed.'

Clearly, the sense of identification was genuine (and, like many a great star, Madonna has no sense of personal identity until she is emulating, or impersonating, someone else), but there were other reasons for desperately wanting, or needing, the part.

Chapter Twenty-Four

Though Madonna's star had continued to rise, she had also found herself trapped in an artistic cul-de-sac and, at the same time, the career she most wanted – to be a major movie star – had continued to elude her. Since her striking debut in *Desperately Seeking Susan* (1985), her movie career had floundered. *Shanghai Surprise* (1986), produced by the former Beatle George Harrison's Handmade Films and co-starring Sean Penn, was an unmitigated disaster that encouraged howls of derision from the critics. In *Who's That Girl?* (1987), a comedy in which she plays a thieving blonde who bullies a nerdish lawyer (Griffin Dunne) into helping her take revenge against thugs who got her jailed for a murder she did not commit, she attempted, dismally, to imitate Judy Holliday and received another critical drubbing. This was followed by a short role as a 1930s nightclub singer in one of the four stories in Howard Brookner's *Bloodhounds of Broadway* (1989), an anachronistic interweaving of four of Damon Runyon's famous short stories about New Year's Eve on Broadway in 1928. This also failed dismally at the box office and did little to further her career. The combination of her widely publicised affair with Warren Beatty, her role as Breathless Mahoney in Beatty's successful *Dick Tracy* (1990), and her Blonde Ambition Tour, cleverly timed to tie in with the release of Beatty's movie, placed her back in the moviegoer's eye, but the critics took the general view that her Breathless Mahoney was no more than another impersonation of Marilyn Monroe. This jaundiced view was only confirmed when she performed 'Sooner or Later (I Always Get My Man)' at the 1991 Academy Awards show, looking like a Marilyn Monroe double. And though Madonna had penned some of the songs for the movie, it was Stephen Sondheim's 'Sooner or Later', ironically sung by Madonna-as-Marilyn, that won the Best Original Song Oscar.

Other movie appearances followed, but with the exception of the execrable *Body of Evidence* (1992), none were starring roles. Though Madonna was convincing as the sharp-tongued, gum-chewing, sexually promiscuous Mae in Penny Marshall's *A League of Their Own* (1991), about a women's baseball team during World War Two, the role was minor and did little to enhance her movie career. Thereafter, given the débâcle of *Body of Evidence*, she was reduced to being hardly more than a 'guest star' in various minor movies, including Abel Ferrara's *Snake Eyes* (1993), the Allison Anders short, *The Missing Ingredient*, in the four-part feature *Four Rooms* (1995) and Wayne Wang's amiably eccentric *Blue in the Face* (1996), in which she pops up as a singing telegram girl.

Simultaneously, her pop career had led her into an artistic cul-de-sac from where there appeared to be no way forward. A career based on the outrageous, on deliberately cultivated controversy, can only run so far and already Madonna was in trouble. The need to be outrageous had forced her to ever more shocking performances, all depending on superb physical fitness, athletic ability and shameless exhibitionism, rather than on her singing ability. For the *Who's That*

Girl? world tour, she replaced her 'slut rock queen' and 'boy toy' images with clinging black corsets and fishnet stockings, and encouraged the obscene outcries of male fans ('Show us your tits!') by becoming ever more blatantly sexual on stage.

Still the need to shock continued.

Striking up a close friendship with the equally outrageous stand-up comic, Sandra Bernhard (known as 'the Mouth that Roars'), Madonna zealously played up to all the talk about their real or widely imagined lesbian relationship. When she formed her own company, Madonna Incorporated, its three major divisions were named Boy-Toy (the music business), Slutco (the videos) and Siren (the films). In March 1989, shortly after signing a $5 million Pepsi Cola deal for one of the largest media campaigns ever orchestrated, she premièred her controversial 'Like a Prayer' video on MTV. In the video, she appears mostly in a black slip, gyrating sensually in front of a field of burning crosses, writhing erotically on a pew in a church, kissing the statue of a black saint, becoming afflicted with bleeding nail wounds in the palms of her hands, dancing uninhibitedly with a gospel troupe and, finally, kneeling before one of the gospel singers as if being blessed by him while her breasts heave dramatically in her uplift bra. Accusations of blasphemy predictably filled the media and Pepsi instantly cancelled their massively hyped commercial.

Not content with this, Madonna followed it with her 'Express Yourself' video. Described by an unofficial biographer, Douglas Thompson, as a 'carnal mini-movie all about making love not money', it shows Madonna in black stockings, corset and suspenders, rolling her stomach, grabbing her crotch and lapping up a saucer of milk while chained to a bed. Given that Madonna's fans consisted largely of pubescent girls and adolescent boys, such antics were viewed with increasing alarm by the public and media alike. Not to be fazed, Madonna, when awarded the Bad Taste Attention award, responded by appearing on the Arsenio Hall talk show where she informed the live audience and, thus, the nation, how much she liked to receive an erotic spanking.

By the time of the Blonde Ambition Tour of 1990, she was into conical bras, sci-fi bustiers, crucifixes, cross-dressing, simulated masturbation, and a lot of on-stage talk about spanking and other previously taboo sexual subjects. This was followed by the 'Justify My Love' video, leaning heavily on Nazi fetishism. Wearing scant black lingerie and sky-scraper heels, Madonna performed with her customary athleticism, but also kissed and nuzzled the model Amanda Cazalet, surrounded herself with male dancers in fishnet stockings and leather, gyrating against women in suspenders with nipples exposed, and generally suggested the pleasures of every imaginable fetish, including S&M, voyeurism, bisexuality, group sex and cross-dressing. The video was banned by MTV and not allowed to be shown in Britain until after 9 p.m., but it became the first video single ever released and a worldwide *cause celebre* and bestseller.

This *succès de scandale*, combined with a movie career that was increasingly being viewed as a bad joke, turned into Madonna's artistic cul-de-sac and made her look to Evita for salvation.

Chapter Twenty-Five

While Madonna's artfully produced videos and stage productions were causing outrage and gaining her worldwide media attention, her private life was doing much the same. Given the blurring between facts and fantasy engendered by stars of her magnitude, it was no surprise that the public at large widely believed her to be an immoral woman who fearlessly lived outside normal moral constraints. This view of her was only made more concrete when, in 1985, she met and fell in love with the volatile, dangerous actor Sean Penn.

The son of Leo Penn, an actor turned television producer, and Eileen Ryan, a former Broadway star, Sean Penn was brought up with a younger brother in Malibu and went into acting at an early age. Getting his big break opposite Tim Hutton in *Taps*, he went on to act in a string of impressive movies while also showing himself to have a violent and self-destructive streak. By the time he had made *The Falcon and the Snowman*, which is when he first met Madonna, he already had a reputation for beating up people, especially press photographers.

The affair between Madonna and Penn was passionate in the extreme and erupted just when Madonna had become the focus of almost obsessive media attention. Given Penn's hatred of the press, there was bound to be trouble – which indeed there was. Photographers were punched out, cameras were smashed, and more than one legal writ was issued.

Soon Madonna and Penn were being treated like the Liz Taylor and Richard Burton of the 1980s, though more often dubbed the 'poison Penns'.

On 16 August 1985, in a flamboyant ceremony which Penn described as the remaking of *Apocalypse Now*, Madonna, aged twenty-six, and Penn, twenty-five, were married and the media circus almost turned into a nightmare, with Madonna giving the finger to the newspaper helicopters buzzing low overhead, drowning out the words of the ceremony, and Penn growing red-faced with rage.

Surviving their wedding day, the supposedly happy couple honeymooned for the following four days in the Highlands Inn in Carmel, then moved into a $3.5 million Bel Air estate, protected by an electrified fence and high walls topped with steel spikes. Penn threatened to install machine-gun towers on those same walls to keep the press photographers at bay.

Within a matter of weeks there were rumours that the marriage was in desperate straits and that Madonna had sought psychiatric help.

Continuing to swear at and attack press photographers, Penn was charged more than once with assault. During the making of *Shanghai Surprise*, in which he played a down-at-heel adventurer in love with Madonna's unlikely 1930s missionary, he karate-chopped and kicked one of Macao's more eminent journalists and in general made trouble right down the line. Back in the United States, after the completion of filming, he violently attacked the singer/songwriter David Wolinski and was subsequently prosecuted by the Los Angeles City Attorney. Though fined $1,700 and placed on a year's probation, he continued to attack journalists and photographers laying seige to Madonna and eventually ended up in jail for reckless driving and other parole violations.

Though publicly standing by her man, Madonna had privately decided to end the marriage. While Penn served his thirty-two day sentence in the jail of Bridgeport in California's Mono County, Madonna toured Japan, the United States and Europe, turning herself into the hottest woman in show business and, eventually, like her heroine, Evita, into one of the world's most revered *and* despised women. By the time she returned to America, Penn was out of prison and bombarding her with desperate phone calls.

Convinced that she was pregnant, Madonna decided to stick with Penn. Upon learning that she was *not* pregnant, she served him divorce papers. When Penn started behaving decently, she took him back again. As soon as he was home, Penn returned to his old ways, screaming abuse and beating up photographers.

Suddenly, Madonna began talking in public about her morbid fears of dying from cancer like her mother and, of course, like Evita, whom she still desperately wished to portray in the on-and-off movie version of the legendary stage musical.

When her fears about breast cancer were laid to rest (sighs of relief from her vast public, deeply grateful that she was neither pregnant nor dying from cancer) she decided to prove her worth as a 'serious' actress, thus as a contender for the Evita role, by playing the secretary, Karen, in Pulitzer-prize-winning David Mamet's three-character drama, *Speed-the-Plow*, which premièred at the Royal Theater in New York on 3 May 1988.

After auditioning with more than 300 other actresses and then rehearsing for six weeks, Madonna took to the stage wearing dark hair, a 'sensible' skirt, spectacles and low-heeled shoes – a far cry from the glamorous woman normally seen by her adoring or sneering public. However, her attempt to be 'serious', though admirable, failed to impress the critics and she soon returned to her outrageous pop career and growing marital problems.

The public and media interest in the marriage of the 'poison Penns' was not abated by Madonna's growing friendship with the outrageous, reportedly lesbian, Sandra Bernhard. Indeed, Bernhard was now contributing to the gossip by making saucy jokes about the friendship and continuing to imply that she and Madonna had their own 'special' relationship.

Enraged on both counts, Penn became more violent, bawled abuse at Madonna in public, argued constantly at home, kicked down doors and punched out walls, hid guns all around the house and threatened to use them against invading journalists.

Finally, when he heard that Madonna had won the role of Breathless Mahoney in Warren Beatty's *Dick Tracy* and was, even worse, having an affair with the ageing though still notorious Lothario, Penn broke into his own home, attacked Madonna, tied her to a chair and allegedly screamed abuse and assaulted her.

Though the exact nature of that assault is not known, an unofficial Madonna biographer, Douglas Thompson (*Madonna Revealed*), quotes Police Lieutenant Bill McSweeney, who was present at the Malibu Sheriff's Department when Madonna, having made her escape, appeared with a cut lip and her eyes streaked with tears, to describe what had happened during her hours of imprisonment by Sean Penn. Proscribed by law from describing the violation in detail, McSweeney would only say that it was 'a unique, specific type of violence' and 'a serious matter'.

Penn was lucky. Deciding to avoid the media circus that would inevitably result if she took Penn to court, Madonna refused to press charges and instead, on 5 January 1989, filed for divorce. After agreeing to a division of their property, she left their Malibu home and moved into a heavily guarded house in Hollywood.

However, subsequent rumours about exactly what kind of humiliation had been inflicted on Madonna during that terrible, final night with Sean Penn, combined with Madonna's ongoing image as the bad girl of pop music and her widely reported affair with Warren Beatty, only heightened her notoriety – and yet again, despite what she had been through, she seemed determined to exploit it ruthlessly.

In 1991, *Truth or Dare* (British title: *In Bed With Madonna*) was released to a virtual avalanche of condemnation. A no-holds-barred documentary on Madonna backstage and at home, it seems, even after the 'Like a Prayer' video and the Blonde Ambition Tour, almost wilfully perverse, or childish, in its need to deliberately shock. During the course of the documentary, Madonna shows how she 'gives head' with the aid of a bottle of Evian water, sings a song about farting, bawls that she's 'getting a hard-on' while she ogles two of the male performers, rips off the clothes of one of her male dancers shouting, 'Your cock is big!' and throws another dancer out of her bed with the comment: 'Don't come back until your cock is bigger'. She also engages in the by now customary lesbian innuendo with Sarah Bernhard; stretches out melodramatically on her mother's grave as if wanting to hug the corpse; and insultingly sticks her fingers down her throat, indicating nausea to her gathered friends, including Warren Beatty, when the actor Kevin Costner leaves her dressing room, having just told her that her performance on stage was 'neat'.

The pornographic nature of much of *Truth or Dare* was followed more blatantly in 1992 with the release of the feature film, *Body of Evidence*, in which Madonna had her final starring role to date, but in a 'thriller' that many assessed as little more than yet another of her thinly disguised exercises in calculated, pornographic outrage. The movie died at the box office and was rushed very quickly into video.

Eventually reaching what must be viewed as the last outpost of calculated bad taste, in 1992, Madonna's book, *Sex*, was published to unprecedented hype. A doormat-sized tome with spiral binding and aluminium covers, wrapped in firmly sealed polythene to prevent browsing, *Sex*, when prised open, presents us with a collection of glossy, black-and-white photographs of Madonna and others, semi-nude and completely nude, engaging in sexual posing or activities. Designed deliberately to shock and promoted as such (hence the plain, sealed wrapping), the photos show Madonna as a (more or less) straight pin-up – half nude in a pizza parlour, being gawped at by the clientele; standing on a kerbside, holding a handbag, smoking a cigarette, and naked except for high heels – but it also plays out a variety of sleazier, darker fantasies, photographed in gloomy basement toilets containing religious bricabrac (the crosses and candles so familiar from Madonna's videos) and in cheap hotel rooms. The fantasies, to which Madonna contributes her own explanatory prose, feature male and female gays, sado-masochists, leather-clad, knife-wielding

Hispanics and blacks, cross-dressers, androgynes, a belly-up Alsatian (over which Madonna leans suggestively) and even tattooed skinheads whose genitals are pierced with pins and rings. Gang rape, sexual threats with knives and an orgy in which a musician has sex with his sister (and, we must assume, with Madonna) are clearly suggested.

Madonna's supportive text is similarly outrageous – or attempts to be so – taking the form of handwritten or printed prose in which she recounts her erotic dreams, describes a real or imagined lesbian relationship; boasts of her own 'gushing' orgasms; discusses her own genitalia; and praises the pleasures of sodomy and bondage.

As anticipated, *Sex* was widely condemned and thus received immense, helpful publicity. This time, however, the desire to shock backfired. Many of Madonna's 'wannabes' (the pubescent girls who 'wanna be' like Madonna) felt ostracised by the book's relentless, uncomfortably *adult* perversity and responded by deserting her for good. More mature observers, on the other hand, particularly when informed that *Sex* was 'meant to be funny', felt that it was, along with *Truth or Dare* and *Body of Evidence*, no more than a desperate attempt by an ageing superstar to top what she had previously done and revitalise an almost exhausted oeuvre – one based on outrage.

Clearly, then, Madonna was at an impasse and had to do something to correct the situation.

Like Evita, Madonna had recreated herself and controlled her public image through a ruthless manipulation of the press. She had created 'Madonna' as deliberately as Eva Duarte had created '*Santa* Evita'. She managed this by creating her own world,

Madonna Incorporated, which, not unlike Evita's Buenos Aires empire, was, and is, a corporation run on total obedience, with its workers forced to sign what amounts to a Madonna Secrets Act that prevents them from talking on the record.

Madonna Incorporated is the umbrella organisation for three highly organised companies: Boy Toy, which controls everything to do with Madonna's music business; Slutco, for the creation of Madonna's promotional and commercial videos; and Siren, which is tasked with finding and developing movies suitable for Madonna. The overall function of Madonna Incorporated is to carefully control Madonna's ever-changing image (accurately described by the British writer Martin Amis as 'baby-doll, dominatrix, flower-child, vamp'; to which we can now add Barbarella and pop diva) and maximise its financial potential, through music, videos, stage performances and movies, to the absolute limit.

The extent to which this ever-changing image is controlled can be gauged in the extraordinary demands that Madonna Incorporated makes on those who wish to interview her or photograph her. Anyone, no matter how important, who refuses to meet Madonna's remarkably stringent (some say 'impossible' or 'outrageous') demands is unlikely to get anywhere near her.

As an example, when Madonna's notorious *Sex* book was published, even the acclaimed Martin Amis was refused an interview, most likely because his own fame could have led to the published work being read as a 'Martin Amis interview' rather than an 'interview with Madonna'. (It is also possible that Amis was viewed as someone who would not be content to become an unpaid PR pen-pusher for Madonna, but would write his own, possibly disagreeable, thing.) So, instead of the expected interview, Amis was invited to fly all the way from London to New York for no more than a sixty-minute perusal of the book, under the watchful eye of an editor, with the taking of notes forbidden, after being compelled to sign 'a long and menacing legal agreement', in an office on the tenth floor of Time–Warner, Sixth Avenue. It is a tribute to the pulling power of Madonna that Amis actually agreed to this.

Like Evita, therefore, Madonna has created her own world and rules it with an iron fist. As the revealing *Truth or Dare* (*In Bed With Madonna*) documentary has shown, Madonna is a mixture of 'Woman with the Whip' and '*Santa* Evita': cruel one minute, kind the next; on the one hand taking a materialistic interest in those surrounding her; on the other, dealing ruthlessly with them should they make the mistake of displeasing her. Madonna is a power unto herself, just as Evita was.

Nevertheless, for all her material success and power, the *Sex* book had placed her at the end of a track that could go no farther, had rebounded miserably upon her, and had damaged her credibility as a serious artist. Her stage performances had gone just about as far as staged erotica could go and would not be helped in the future by her advancing age and the audience's Pavlovian demands for ever more outrageous, or controversial, performances. Unable, for those reasons, to continue as the 'slut queen' of pop, she had either to take a more orthodox route – romantic ballads and diva performances – or, even better, win the most sought-after role in movie-musical history and prove that she could conquer the silver screen.

That role is Evita, and Madonna, who desperately wanted it and now needs it, has finally won it.

In fact, she had been pursuing the role for years.

Chapter Twenty-Six

As far back as 1985, when her soft-porn video, *A Certain Sacrifice*, was going on sale in video stores, Madonna was meeting secretly with Robert Stigwood, the Australian producer who had staged the show in London, in the hope of winning the title role in *Evita*. However, Stigwood hired Ken Russell to direct the movie and Russell insisted on having Liza Minnelli, instead of the original, highly acclaimed Evita, Elaine Page. Minnelli's London test recording was considered a 'disaster', Minnelli herself insisted that the tape be destroyed, and Ken Russell and Robert Stigwood eventually parted company.

In 1989, the film director Oliver Stone, on a hot roll after *Platoon* and *Wall Street*, announced that he would be making the $20 million musical and was considering such high-fliers as Barbra Streisand, Meryl Streep and Madonna for the lead role. The parts of Juan Perón and Ché Guevara had not yet been cast, though the press announced that Patrick Swayze had been rejected by Stone for the part of Ché, despite spending a small fortune on demos.

Madonna approached Stone for the part of Evita, but she refused to take the screen test insisted upon by him, and also insisted on having Sean Penn as Ché

Turning her down on both counts, Stone met Meryl Streep, a classically trained singer and award-winning actress, and decided to give her the role. While Stone completed his screenplay, Streep took singing and dancing lessons, and also taped a selection of songs from the score. Andrew Lloyd Webber and Tim Rice were not convinced by Streep's singing, so Streep was rejected after a year of hard work and Stone went on to other projects, leaving *Evita* free again.

Madonna then stepped back into the picture.

Ever since the success of Warren Beatty's *Dick Tracy* and the highly effective merchandising package that had gone with it, including Madonna's sound-track album, she and Jeffrey Katzenberg of the Disney studios had kept in close touch. By May 1991 the press was reporting that Katzenberg had managed to put together a new *Evita* package, to be directed by Glenn Gordon (*Clean and Sober*) Caron from his own screenplay and to star Madonna, with Jeremy Irons as Juan Perón and the rap star, Vanilla Ice, tipped as a possible Ché Guevara.

Caron, Irons and Vanilla Ice all dropped out of sight and by July the press were claiming that Madonna's 'long-awaited *Evita* film' was to be ditched by the Disney Studio because of its rocketing budget.

During the following month, Madonna gave a series of interviews in which she more or less sub-stantiated these events, but insisted that, when the problems had been ironed out, she would still be play-ing the role.

A few weeks later, in September, it was announced that an independent film company (not named) had stumped up the required budget (now up from $20 million to $30 million), that Madonna was still tak-ing the starring role, and that shooting would start at locations in Europe early the following year.

Filming did not, as promised, start in 1992 and

another two years would pass before, in March 1994, it was announced that the Disney Studios' production of *Evita* was 'doomed' and the Spanish heart-throb Antonio Banderas was publicly lamenting the fact that he would not be playing Ché Guevara opposite Madonna's Evita Perón.

Approximately six months later, however, the media were excitedly reporting that the famed director Alan Parker had been signed up to direct the movie with Michelle Pfeiffer picked to play Evita, though the Spanish warbler Julio Iglesias (Oliver Stone's original choice for the role of Ché) had received the boot. Michelle Pfeiffer either dropped out of, or was dropped from, the project and *Evita* was in limbo again.

No more was heard of the project until September 1995 when various press reports were insisting that Madonna was still relentlessly pursuing her role and attempting to persuade John (*Saturday Night Fever/Pulp Fiction*) Travolta to co-star as Ché.

In fact, by this time a new $60 million (£39.2 million) *Evita* package had been put together by the producer Andrew Vajna (a Robert Stigwood Organisation/Dirty Hands Production/Cinergi Productions) with Madonna as Evita, Britain's Jonathan Pryce as Juan Perón, the Spanish heart-throb Antonio Banderas as Ché, and Alan Parker as director.

In late 1995, Madonna flew to London to record the soundtrack and in February 1996, filming of the actual movie began, at long last, in Argentina.

Chapter Twenty-Seven

The success of the *Evita* movie is virtually guaranteed. For a start, the original Andrew Lloyd Webber–Tim Rice stage musical was a huge success and remains exceptionally newsworthy. Regarding the film version, Alan Parker, as director, has an impressive track record of movies that are simultaneously commercial, daring, provocative and critically successful.

Parker's first full-length movie, *Bugsy Malone* (1975), a 'musical' with children dressed up and acting as adults, was the official British entry at the Cannes Film Festival, winning eight British Academy nominations and five Stella Awards. *Midnight Express* (1977), his controversial blockbuster about a Turkish prison, won two Academy Awards and four other nominations, including one for Parker as Best Director. *Fame* (1979), a naturalistic musical set in a New York musical college, won two Academy Awards, six nominations and four Golden Globe nominations. *Birdy* (1984), the bizarre story of a traumatised Vietnam vet who thinks he can fly, based on the acclaimed William Wharton novel, won the Grand Prix Special Jury Prize at the Cannes Film Festival. *Mississippi Burning* (1988), a civil rights drama based on a true story, was nominated for seven Academy Awards including Best Director, winning an Award for Best Cinematography. For his directing of the film, Parker was awarded the D.W. Griffith Award by the National Board of Review. The film was nominated for five British Academy Awards, winning three. It also won the Silver Bear at the Berlin Film Festival.

In 1985 Parker was honoured, with the producer Alan Marshall, by the British Academy with the prestigious Michael Balcon Award for Outstanding Contribution to Cinema. Parker is also a founding member and vice-chairman of the Directors' Guild of Great Britain and a member of the British Screen Advisory Council.

The controversial nature of *Evita* – and Madonna's role in it – is not likely to bother this particular director. In fact, he is just as likely to thrive on it. A man of broad creative experience who came up the hard way, he will not be fazed by Madonna's superstar status and will, indeed, probably have good reasons for admiring certain aspects of both Evita and the woman finally chosen to play her. In other words, like both Evita and Madonna, Alan Parker is self-made.

Born to working-class parents in Islington, North London, in 1944, Parker started as a post boy in an advertising firm, soon persuaded them to let him write ads, then moved on to become a full-time copywriter and, eventually, the director of commercials. He started directing at twenty-six. With his friend Alan Marshall (later the co-producer of *Midnight Express*) he formed the Alan Parker Film Company, which made over 500 commercials. He inched into movies, first by writing the screenplay for a feature film, *Melody* (1972), then by directing a fifty-minute TV drama, *No Hard Feelings* (1972), and two thirty-minute cinema shorts for EMI: *Our Cissy* and *Footsteps* (both produced in 1973). A subsequent BBC TV special, *The Evacuees* (1974), written by Jack Rosenthal, won the International Emmy Award and a Stella from BAFTA.

Parker is no stranger to controversy. His first cinema feature, *Bugsy Malone* (1975), apart from winning many awards and being an international box-office success, was condemned for exploiting children in adult roles which, particularly in the case of the then child star Jodie Foster, struck many as being uncomfortably sexual. *Midnight Express*, while being critically acclaimed, was also widely condemned for its rewriting of the facts and its xenophobic view of the Turkish authorities. In 1984, to celebrate British Film Year, Parker wrote and directed the provocative documentary *A Turnip Head's Guide to the British Cinema*, in which he expressed his fiercely independent views and lambasted the British film establishment and film critics. His next movie, *Angel Heart* (1986), starring Mickey Rourke, Robert de Niro and Lisa Bonet, opened to a storm of controversy over its X-rated mixture of violence and eroticism. *Mississippi Burning* (1988), while winning many awards, stirred up another hornet's nest of controversy over what many insisted was a superficial, commercialised treatment of a politically sensitive subject. So, if *Evita* is a controversial movie, Parker's the man to direct it.

More importantly, however, he is probably the only living director who can still produce successful film musicals, let alone *unlikely* musicals (which *Evita* clearly is) for the contemporary cinemagoing audience, as his *Bugsy Malone* (1975), *Fame* (1979), *The Wall* (1982) and *The Commitments* (1991) clearly proved. The combination of Parker, Madonna and *Evita* could therefore be magical.

It also has to be said that, while Jonathan Pryce, playing Juan Perón, is one of Britain's finest actors and will almost undoubtedly make a meal of the part and possibly create a great character, it is Antonio Banderas as Ché Guevara who will – and has already started to – create a media sensation.

José Antonio Banderas is unusual in that he is one of the few Spanish heart-throbs to make it to Hollywood stardom. Born in Malaga, Spain, in 1960, he attended the School of Dramatic Arts in his home town, then moved to Madrid, where he performed in a series of stage productions, including the classic Spanish play, *La Historia de los Tarantos* (a gypsy version of *Romeo and Juliet*) and *The Life of Edward the Second*, directed by Luis Pascual.

A physically graceful young man with striking good looks, he was soon picked out by the Spanish director Pedro Almódovar and performed in a number of Almódovar's sensational, sexually explicit movies, including his debut, *Labyrinths of Passion* (1982), *Law of Desire* (1985), the internationally acclaimed *Women on the Verge of a Nervous Breakdown* (1988) and the controversial *Tie Me Up, Tie Me Down* (1990). His string of Spanish movies, many made by other directors, including Carlos Saura, ended with *La Bianca Paloma*, for which Banderas won the Best Actor Award at the Valladolid Film Festival.

Called to Hollywood, Banderas was used not only as an 'action hero' in the likes of Sylvester Stallone's *Assassins* and Robert Rodriguez's *Desperado*, but also as a serious actor, albeit of the matinée idol variety, in a string of artistically prestigious or highly commercial productions, including *The Mambo Kings* (1993) with Armand Assante; the award-winning *Philadelphia* (1994) with Tom Hanks; *The House of the Spirits* (1994) with Meryl Streep, Jeremy

Irons, Glenn Close and Winona Ryder; and *Interview with the Vampire* (1995) with Tom Cruise and Brad Pitt. Within eighteen months, Banderas had become one of the hottest 'new' stars in Hollywood.

Nevertheless, Banderas is not creating a media sensation with *Evita* just because he is the hottest Spanish actor working in movies at the moment. Rather, it is because he featured in Madonna's notorious documentary *Truth or Dare* (*In Bed With Madonna*) as the only man to have publicly rejected her.

Part of *Truth or Dare* was shot in Madrid, where Madonna was then performing on stage. In an attempt to add spice to her documentary, she had herself filmed meeting Banderas at a post-concert bash at the Palace Hotel, Madrid, and made it clear that she had the hots for him and wanted to date him. Banderas, on camera, politely but firmly rejected her on the grounds that he was married – to the lovely actress, Ana Leza, no less.

The Spanish press leapt upon this, turning it into a huge joke, playing repeatedly with headlines such as 'Not even Madonna is infallible'. (This is a pointed, very Spanish reference to the 'infallibility' of the Virgin Mary who, as the Holy Mother, is also called the Madonna.) The joke worked in Spain and the story carried over to the United States where, even before the release of Madonna's documentary, word of mouth about the rejection turned Banderas into an odd folk hero.

Banderas, the love object of thousands of women, had publicly rejected the woman they most loathed in favour of his beloved wife. This made him, in the eyes of his fans, both European and American, even more desirable.

However, even as the Madonna rejection was still warming the hearts of Banderas's fans, he was creating another media blizzard by dumping the wife he was supposed to love so deeply. In the event, he did not do this for Madonna, but for the troubled movie actress Melanie Griffith, with whom he had just made his latest movie, *Two Much*.

Griffith, the daughter of the Alfred Hitchcock heroine, Tippi Hedren, was a former Hollywood 'nymphet' in the likes of *Night Moves* and *Body Double*; became a 'star' with *Working Girl*, for which she was nominated for an Academy Award; and received a lot of press attention, not for her acting but for her widely publicised addiction to alcohol and cocaine. She became involved with Banderas when she was still the wife of Don (*Miami Vice*) Johnson, TV heart-throb, less successful movie actor, occasional ballad crooner, and short-lived lover of Barbra Streisand, who had, ironically, once been in the running to play Evita.

In ditching his wife of nine years, Banderas outraged many of his fans, caused another media sensation, and turned himself, almost overnight, into a major Hollywood star.

The international press therefore loved the Madonna–Banderas–*Evita* story and were beside themselves in print when, in October 1995, Melanie Griffith announced that she would not be working for the first ten weeks of 1996 but would, instead, be flying to Argentina to stay with Banderas until he had completed his role opposite Madonna.

Practically gloating, the hacks reminded their readers of Madonna's previous pursuit of Banderas, his firm rejection of her, and the clear concern of his present girlfriend, Melanie Griffith (previously married to the actor Steven Bauer; twice married to Don Johnson); and that Madonna, in the heady atmosphere of a film set, might make a play for him again. Griffith, they pointed out, was pregnant by Banderas and may have deliberately put herself in that condition to ensnare her gorgeous Spanish lover. Banderas, they suggested, could therefore still be a target for the voracious Madonna – so, clearly, Griffith was flying off to Argentina to protect her man from the evil witch.

In May 1996, as the shooting of *Evita* was being concluded, Melanie Griffith, after divorcing Don Johnson for the second time, married Antonio Banderas.

The whole affair is a marketing man's dream – particularly with regard to the *Evita* movie – and it looks set to run and run.

Finally, however, the real success of the film will be preordained because of the enormous amount of publicity to be gained from the international outrage already being generated by the very idea of the 'notorious' Madonna playing the 'saintly' Evita.

Oliver Stone had already faced strong Argentinian resistance back in 1989 when he had announced that he was making the movie with Meryl Streep starring. Though Streep is an actress with a serious reputation, the Argentinians were not impressed and caused such a stir that Stone decided to move production from Argentina to Spain. As we have seen, Stone's production went into turnaround, but an even angrier reaction came from Argentina when it was announced that the movie was definitely going into production and that Madonna had won the title role.

Of all the American actresses to be chosen to play

'Saint' Evita, none could have been more inflammatory to the Argentinians than this most controversial and, as many would have it, pornographic of all popular female singers. Their Evita was a 'madonna'; this American Madonna was, in their view, a tramp.

'The musical is a libellous interpretation of Evita's life,' said President Carlos Menem. 'The masses who still believe Evita was a true martyr are not going to tolerate it.'

The European press, energetically gunning for Madonna-as-Evita, had already gleefully reported Sir Andrew Lloyd Webber's criticism that she could not hit the high notes and so had shifted the score down a key. Bearing in mind that Sir Andrew is notorious for the last-minute ditching of his leading ladies and had, indeed, recently caused a show-business scandal and legal row with Faye Dunaway by unceremoniously sacking her from his stage production of *Sunset Boulevard*, the press were eagerly anticipating a similar sacking of Madonna. In fact, Sir Andrew defended her by pointing out that it was 'quite common' to change the score to fit a singer's capabilities and that Madonna was definitely keeping the part. Nevertheless, the press continued to revel in reports of Argentinian anger over Madonna in the role, with particular emphasis on their view of her 'blasphemous' and 'pornographic' sexual image.

Since the corrupt Evita had been turned into a 'madonna' in her own country, it was axiomatic that the Argentinians, with no knowledge of the screenplay, would view Madonna as 'a symbol of prostitution' and accuse her of playing Evita as 'a power-hungry nymphomaniac'.

The British were not much better, with one well-known journalist, Michael Sheridan, even going so far as to compare Madonna (in relation to a rumour that she had repeatedly lit candles and prayed for the role) to 'a brothel queen lusting after the role of a mother superior'. Sheridan, like many other hacks, was derisory about Madonna's acting talents, sneering that she had 'failed, not miserably but squirmingly, cringingly' while failing to mention her striking movie debut in *Desperately Seeking Susan* and her credible work in *Dick Tracy* and *A League of Their Own*. Also, in company with his fellow hacks, he took the Argentinian line that Madonna, by the very nature of her public image, was not morally fit for the role.

'How in Eva's name,' Sheridan asks pompously, 'can this peroxide sex bomb have any credible claim to the celluloid recreation of a great Argentinian lady?'

Indeed, Sheridan was not alone in bending the truths of history in order to get at Madonna. Just like the Argentinians, the Western media conveniently forgot Evita's corruption and cruelty, the bleeding dry of her own country, the hiding away of untold wealth, the assassinations and torture, and instead rewrote her as a living legend and 'saint' – a veritable 'madonna' – who came out of the slums, never forgot her humble origins, and brought comfort and hope to her worshipful workers.

The avalanche of condemnation rolled on and grew worse when the movie company arrived in Argentina to begin the shoot.

By April 1996, *Premier* magazine was reporting that Madonna, no stranger to threats because of her controversial career, was being 'threatened by an entire *nation* as angry Argentinians protested at the singer's arrival in their country to play national heroine Eva Perón . . .' The *Premier* article went on to mine a common vein in the media by stating that the Argentinians were upset not only by the original musical – which had painted Evita as 'a slum girl who slept her way to the top – but, more importantly (or insultingly), because Evita was to be played by 'a woman they consider to be little more than a harlot'.

Madonna's arrival in Argentina had indeed caused a public outcry, with banners stating 'Madonna go home!' and 'Viva Evita! Out with Madonna!' strung across roads leading into Buenos Aires from the airport, anti-Madonna graffiti mushrooming all over the city, old-guard Peronists in the Argentinian Parliament putting forth motions that anyone involved in the production should be declared *persona non grata*; the director Alan Parker refused permission to shoot in important government buildings; and, as a final slap in the face, Argentinian television juxtaposing old newsreel clips of Evita administering to the poor with extracts from Madonna's 'pornographic' videos. Shortly after those broadcasts, at a 'protest camp' near the production, Clara Marin, a former secretary of Evita Perón, allegedly told reporters that the protestors wanted Madonna dead and that if she did not leave Argentina they would kill her. This 'death threat' soon became a wave of 'death threats' that were reported worldwide.

Given her fondness for, and talent for, generating huge controversy, Madonna could not have planned it better herself.

Interestingly enough, even as Madonna's manager, Freddy Demann, was telling *Variety* that he was 'one minute away from pulling her out of that country', *Evita*'s producer, Andrew Vajna, was insisting that reports of death threats had been fabricated and that 'the only Argentinians besieging Madonna are her fans.'

Madonna, meanwhile, was talking – if not to the press, which she was generally avoiding, then at least to President Menem, in the company of Alan Parker, Jonathan Pryce and Antonio Banderas, insisting that she would not 'insult' the memory of Evita and was pleased to be portraying such a 'great and inspiring' woman. ('Her perseverance,' Parker said, 'was incredible.') Charmed and convinced, Menem rescinded his ban on the use of the Casa Rosada (the Presidential Mansion, or Government House) for the shooting of the all-important 'Don't Cry For Me Argentina' scene and allowed Parker, Madonna, Jonathan Pryce, plus three cameras and the camera crews, to do the necessary. Subsequently, on the evening of 10 March 1996, Madonna, as Evita, standing beside Jonathan Pryce (Juan Perón), sang from the balcony of the Casa Rosada to the hundreds of worshipful fans gathered together in the Plaza de Mayo, all pretending to be faithful *descamisados* and roaring their approval on cue.

This, however, did not appease the members of the press, who were increasingly incensed that Madonna was living in Buenos Aires like a recluse, surrounding herself with bodyguards, generally only socialising with officials who needed to be charmed in order to let the filming proceed, and otherwise refusing to give interviews.

The bandwagon rolled on. By May, when production had moved to Budapest for some vital scenes, it was reported that Madonna had been banned from filming in Budapest's Basilica. Madonna, it was noted, had offended Catholics for years by her use of Christian symbols and crosses in videos and live performances. Now the bishops had struck back and even a reported offer of 60 million forints (£300,000) to film in the sacred building had failed to budge church officials.

'Madonna is an immoral person,' said Endre Foldi, chaplain of the Basilica, 'and her behaviour does not belong in church. The whole world knows what she is like and we cannot humiliate the church or denigrate it by having her naked in the church. Anyone who shows her naked body in front of men is immoral. Everyone in the church agrees with this decision, from Rome down.'

However, Madonna would be allowed to enter to pray as a private individual, the kindly chaplain added.

Matters were not improved by the fact that, just as she had done in Argentina, Madonna made enemies by being too reclusive, usually eating with her bodyguards and venturing out only once or twice to local restaurants, always heavily guarded. Even journalists seeking interviews were reduced to handing one of her many flunkies a written list of questions and waiting outside her suite until the replies, also written out, were handed back by the same, or another, flunky. Naturally, this kind of behaviour outraged the journalists, gained Madonna more bad press, and doubtless fanned the flames of the Budapest 'controversy' over whether or not she should be allowed to film in the Basilica.

(She was not.)

The Budapest controversy was only the latest in many such highly public rows over the production of the film, and more are bound to erupt before filming is finished. At the time of writing (May 1996), filming is nearing completion and the controversy (and invaluable publicity) continues to grow.

In fact, the publicity can only be increased by the news that Madonna, at thirty-seven, was, in May 1996, four months pregnant by her fitness trainer and current boyfriend, Cuban-born Carlos Leon (twenty-nine) and, perhaps more importantly, was also about to publish a $2 million autobiography in which she has promised to show 'a side of Madonna that you haven't seen before'. Reportedly, the revelations include fresh details about her stormy marriage to Sean Penn, her attraction to Tina Turner, her dates with Michael Jackson, her torrid relationship with Prince, her love for Warren Beatty, and even her belief that Elvis Presley died on her 19th birthday for 'a reason' and his soul has since re-emerged in her.

According to friends of Madonna, she planned her pregnancy with 'the precision of a military campaign' and 'chose' Carlos Leon for his body, his genes, and also because she is his boss and was able to make him sign over all rights to the baby. The baby's birth and the publication of the 'tell-all' book have both been timed, whether deliberately or not, to coincide roughly with the release of the *Evita* movie.

Given this, as well as Alan Parker's reputation as a 'controversial' director and Madonna's undiminished passion to make the role her own, the *Evita* movie, even if not a critical success, will almost certainly be a box-office sensation.

'I will return,' Evita had said, 'and I will be millions.'

Resurrected in the shape of Madonna, she might make good that vow.

About the Author

W.A. Harbinson is the author of biographies of Charles Bronson, George C. Scott and Elvis Presley. His book *The Illustrated Elvis* reached No. 1 on the US bestseller lists, selling over one million copies. Harbinson has also written two bestselling novels, *Genesis* and *Revelation*. His controversial non-fiction book, *Project UFO: The Case for Man-Made Flying Saucers*, is published by Boxtree in hardcover and paperback.